IN THE REALM OF

GHOSTS

And Hauntings

IN THE REALM OF

GHOSTS

And Hauntings

E. Randall Floyd

HARBOR
HOUSE

AUGUSTA, GEORGIA

In the Realm of Ghosts and Hauntings
By E. Randall Floyd
A Harbor House Book/ March 2002

For information address:
HARBOR HOUSE
3010 STRATFORD DRIVE
AUGUSTA, GEORGIA 30909

Book Design by Fredna L. Forbes
Front Cover Illustration Artist Unknown
Back Cover Illustration by Robert Forbes

Library of Congress Cataloging- in- Publication Data

Floyd, E. Randall.
  In the Realm of Ghosts & Hauntings / by E. Randall Floyd. -- 1st ed.
      p. cm.
Includes index.
  ISBN 1- 891799- 06- 1
  1. Ghosts. 2. Haunted houses. 3. Apparitions. I. Title.
  BF1461 . F58 2002
  133. 1-- dc21
                                        2002000418
Printed in the United States
10 9 8 7 6 5 4 3 2 1

For Philippa Denny

Contents

INTRODUCTION

Are ghosts for real? Since ancient times a preponderance of people have believed in a realm not far removed from our own three-dimensional world of light and substance, a realm of shifting shadows and disembodied form, a misty, uncharted realm said to be inhabited by the spirits of the dead.

"Who can deny that ghosts walk among us?" asked one famous Greek philosopher. A 15th century German scholar warned: "The {low} world of the dead is a place of rotting flesh and lasting agony, a place to be very much shunned."

The Sumerians might have been the first to write about "gloomy spirits" wandering the earth, but the Greeks and Romans also had their "shades" that foretold future events. Old Kingdom Egyptians worshipped a variety of "underworld" deities and spent much of their time preparing their mortal bodies and souls for spiritual encounters in the afterlife.

Thousands of years earlier, Stone Age hunters retreated deep inside caves to beseech the spirit world for favors. Effigies carved in clay and stone suggest that Neolithic people believed in some form of life after death. Trinkets unearthed in ancient tombs might have been used to ward off evil spirits.

During the Middle Ages, stories about ghosts and hauntings were as common as wars and famine. Nary a village or castle lacked time-honored yarns about dragging chains, wandering wraiths, headless horsemen, or hooded apparitions flitting across moonlit lawns.

Across the ocean, in the wild lands that would one day be known as America, naked savages prayed for protection against fearful entities awaiting them in the boiling blackness of The Pit. Every now and then, these spectral monstrosities would ascend from subterranean realms to wreak havoc among the living.

Even during the so-called Age of Enlightenment, humanist scholars and robed clerics openly embraced the notion of a spirit world, a dark, murky domain inhabited by the phantasmic remnants of those who had already crossed over. Victorian conjurers and mediums resorted to rocking tables and tapping chairs in shabby—some might say dubious—quests to commune with these spirits and unlock secrets from beyond the grave.

Today, as we head into the new millennium, a shockingly high percentage of the American population believes that some form of life continues to exist on the "other side." That would mean, in the purest sense, that they believe in ghosts.

Should we fear ghosts? That, too, is a question that stays with modern man, just as it did with our ancestors down through the ages. The prospect of encountering something that shouldn't be there—something as loathsome and darkly disturbing as a rotting entity rising from a moldy grave—continues to be the stuff of nightmares.

As rational humans, we know that can't happen. Dead is dead. Dust is dust. Once bodies are committed to the earth, they should remain there, grim reminders of the immutability of nature. Yet, many of us do not gleefully stroll past cemeteries late at night or seek out haunted houses to while away the hours.

Ghosts have always filled men with dread and terror.

This age-old fear of phantoms seems to be universal and probably stems from the notion that the dead aren't supposed to walk among the living, that in doing so, they violate some esoteric law of nature.

Ghosts are also painful reminders that life is only a temporary thing. They seem to be saying: "Just as I am, so shall you be."

Whether one believes in ghosts or not, the subject simply will not go away. Like the weather and sex, it seems here to stay. It is a timeless fascination, an energy that knows no bounds. Even without hard evidence either way, some of us believe in ghosts because it seems like a natural extension of an ordered universe. Others believe simply because it is fun.

It seems safe to say we will never know for sure, at least while we count ourselves among the living. So, dear readers, for the time being, let us rejoice that there will always be an audience for Grandma's juicy tales about clanking chains and red-eyed apparitions. Let us pray that fireside yarns will never give way to television, computer games and other forms of modern entertainment.

--E. Randall Floyd
Augusta, Georgia, 2002

Acknowledgements

Writing a book like this requires the input of many people. I want to thank all the writers, researchers and reporters for their valuable and unselfish contributions in helping make this project possible. Some of you know who you are. To all my former and future students and fans, here is a special thanks to you. You know who you are, too. May you continue to read and tell stories and be filled with an undying sense of wonder about our strange and wonderful universe. As always, a sincere thank-you is due my wife, Anne, and my son, Rand, who read most of the original copy and made numerous suggestions. I also want to thank Lynn Forbes for her patience and talented work. I am deeply indebted to my late grandmother, Molly Tillman, a brave pioneering soul who thrilled and chilled me many a night with hair-raising stories about all those colorful spooks and "haints" that inhabited the bleak and monster-filled Altamaha River Swamp in an earlier age. Your stories are as thrilling today as they were back then, and just as real.

ALCATRAZ

Island of lost souls

They called it "The Rock"—a brooding, fortress-like prison perched on a fog-shrouded island in San Francisco Bay.

Until it closed in 1963 and became part of the Golden Gate National Recreation Area, Alcatraz was home to some of the nation's most notorious criminals, including mob boss Al Capone, "Birdman" Robert Strouss and George "Machine Gun" Kelly. Many people believe the spirits of these and other inmates still haunt the infamous prison.

Experts who have investigated paranormal activity on the island claim Alcatraz—or "Hellcatraz" as the inmates called it—might be one of the most haunted places in the world. That's not surprising, given The Rock's bloody history of brutality, torture, madness and death.

Chilling stories have been told about unexplainable crashing sounds, cold spots, unearthly screams and glowing red eyes peering from darkened corridors and long-abandoned cellblocks. Ghosts are said to haunt almost every room, and even a phantom lighthouse has been seen rising out of the murky fog.

Almost every guard and official who served there until it was shut down by Attorney General Robert Kennedy in the early 1960s experienced something out of the ordinary. Today, park rangers who conduct tours occasionally reveal shocking supernatural secrets about the island's tragic past. Many of the more than one million visitors who pay to tour the island each year come away convinced that something evil lurks within the prison's cold, thick walls.

The story of Alcatraz actually begins in ancient times with the Miwok Indians who avoided the island because they believed it was inhabited by evil spirits. Bones and other artifacts excavated from the chalky-white rocks suggest it might have served as a burial ground for outcasts and other undesirables. When they found it in the early 1600s, Spanish explorers named it Alcatraz—"The Island of Pelicans."

Two centuries later, the U.S. Army Corps of Engineers converted the island into an impenetrable concrete fortress. It wasn't long before The Rock claimed its first lives. In 1857, a team of workers digging a roadway perished when a freak landslide buried them alive.

The first prisoners arrived on the island the week before Christmas in 1859. No one knows who they were or the nature of their crimes because all records were lost or destroyed. With the outbreak of Civil War two years later, the secret facility was designated as the U.S. Army's official military prison.

Prisoners sent to The Rock suffered unspeakably. They drank contaminated water, ate one meal a day, slept head to foot in cold, cramped cells. The lack of sanitation facilities led to the outbreak of diseases that took the lives of countless inmates. Adding to their misery were so-called torture chambers — damp, unlit holes carved out of the rocky basement where uncooperative prisoners were beaten and locked up in the dark with rats.

In 1933 the maximum-security prison was turned over to the Federal Bureau of Investigation to house some of the worst elements in society. Within months, Alcatraz was home to hundreds of hardened criminals – thieves, rapists, kidnappers, anarchists, murderers and gangsters such as Capone.

Escape was impossible. Two miles of deep water separated the island from the mainland. If they were lucky enough to get past armed guards with itchy trigger fingers, felons had to face strong riptides and killer sharks—hammerheads and great whites—that cruised silently beneath the dark waves.

Life at Alcatraz was brutal. Beatings were common, as were lockup periods in isolation chambers. In time, The Rock became synonymous with hell. Prisoners knew the only way out was in a pine box.

Lying in their bunks late at night, inmates began to hear strange, whispering sounds. Some told about waking up in the middle of the night and seeing eerie blue lights hovering over their cots. Others saw shimmering forms floating up from the floor and passing through walls. Moaning noises and clanking chains were heard coming from unoccupied cells and chambers.

Particularly disturbing, especially to unseasoned guards, were phantom gun shots and cannon blasts that sent them scurrying for shelter. Every now and then the fire alarm would go off in a deserted laundry room. When guards arrived to put out the fire, billowing clouds of smoke would prevent them from entering the room. Seconds later, the smoke would clear—as if it had never been there.

At first, guards laughed at the stories. Terrified prisoners afraid of the dark were ridiculed—or worse, confined to isolation. The frantic cries of one unfortunate inmate who had been placed in solitary confinement were ignored until it was too late. When guards finally got around to checking on him, he was dead. Strangle marks were found on his neck, even though he had been alone in the cell the whole time.

Before long, prison officials themselves began to notice strange phenomena. Guards making their rounds late at night encountered sad, sobbing sounds. They felt unseen fingers at the back of their necks and frequently encountered "cold spots"—places where, for no apparent reason, temperatures would drop drastically.

Prisoners clad in nineteenth-century clothing were often spotted wandering remote regions of the prison, particularly in Cell Block A and the dungeon area. When guards approached, these apparitions would vanish. One staffer said he watched a gang of shackled inmates marching around in a circle before they disappeared.

The warden—a man named Johnson—heard the unmistakable sound of a woman sobbing while conducting a tour of the facility. An icy wind reportedly blew through the group, frightening many away from the dungeon area.

Do the ghosts of long-dead inmates still roam the old prison? Psychic investigators such as Sylvia Brown and Peter James say yes. They suspect that the disembodied voices and spectral sightings reported at Alcatraz might be all that remain of the tortured souls killed or driven mad during their harsh confinement.

During a visit to the prison, renowned ghost hunter Richard Senate said he felt "icy fingers" on his neck when he visited Al Capone's cell. A psychic who accompanied him sensed an "evil and persistent" presence in Cell 12-D. Both left the island convinced that

Alcatraz was cursed with an unhealthy psychical energy.

Others have told similar stories. On a tour of the facility in 1984, author Michael Kouri said the spirit of a dead prisoner spoke to him during a trance and told him about being beaten and thrown into solitary confinement with both legs broken. A CBS news team reported similar ghostly activities in what was once the therapy room and another in the prison laundry room where at least one prisoner was murdered.

In the early 1990s, a *Sightings* television crew visited the facility and seemed to confirm on video what many psychics and others already knew. The Rock is indeed haunted, they concluded—haunted by the spirits of hundreds of men who suffered long years of abuse, mistreatment and torture at the hands of cruel, uncaring officials.

Some say the hauntings will continue until the prison is torn down and the spirits of those who died there are released.

ALICE FLAGG

Girl's spirit still searches for long-lost ring

Of all the great ghost stories of the Deep South, none is more beguiling than that of Alice Flagg, the beautiful young South Carolina belle whose tormented spirit is said to haunt the lonely marshes and live oak glades surrounding her ancestral homeplace near Pawleys Island.

Since Alice's death more than 140 years ago, scores of people claim to have seen her ghost—usually described as a delicate young woman with luminous brown eyes, long, auburn hair and dressed in a shimmering white gown—floating serenely across the lawn or nearby cemetery at All Saints Church where her body is buried.

Occasionally, she has been seen gliding up the stairs or hovering in front of a mirror in her bedroom. Most witnesses say the frail apparition appears to be clutching her chest, as if searching for the secret engagement ring she once wore around her neck.

One visitor to Alice's home, a sprawling, plantation-style showplace known locally as The Hermitage, swore she awoke one night to find the ghostly form of the long dead girl standing at the foot of her bed. Another said she heard her footsteps going up and down the stairway all night long, while yet another insisted she heard Alice's ghost singing or weeping outside the window late one night.

Among the visitors who claimed to have experienced psychic revelations at The Hermitage were movie actress

Patricia Neal and her husband, writer Roald Dahl.

The story of Alice Flagg began in the mid-nineteenth century when the sixteen-year-old daughter of well-to-do rice planters Ebenezer and Margaret Elizabeth Belin Flagg fell in love with a young timber merchant. Thinking the young man was beneath their social standing, the Flagg family condemned the relationship and encouraged Alice to allow more suitable gentlemen of the gentry class to court her.

"Alice," her brother, Dr. Allard Flagg, cautioned her, "he is not a professional man. He is a common turpentine dealer. Can't you see that the young man is beneath the notice of a Flagg? Let me hear no more about it!"

Ever her mother railed against the relationship: "Alice, every woman must leave her mark on earth. And how can you etch on this earth anything that's worthwhile if you attach yourself to this common lumberman?"

But Alice would have none of that. She loved the young timber man and conspired to meet him whenever possible. She even accepted his engagement ring—though had to conceal it in a ribbon worn around her neck because of her family's strong objections.

It was finally decided that the only way to resolve the situation was to send Alice away to school in Charleston. There the wealthy young heiress would find a suitable beau, a proper mate for marriage.

But Charleston life took its toll on Alice. She abhorred the parties and teas, the endless procession of upper-class young men who tried to woo her favor. Most of all, she missed the man of her dreams back home.

Despondent and lonely, Alice cried herself to sleep each night. She became frail and listless, refusing to leave her room except to eat and attend classes. Her once-beautiful features became waxy and pale, and her beautiful brown eyes no longer glowed.

One night, it was arranged for her to attend a ball at the St. Cecelia Society. At one point she complained about a pain in her left side. She also felt feverish and asked to go home. A physician took note of her condition, did a quick examination and determined that she was suffering from malaria, a common but potentially fatal ailment that struck thousands of people along the Carolina coast each year.

The next day the doctor notified her family. It took her brother four days to reach Charleston by carriage. In that time Alice's condition steadily worsened. By the time Dr. Flagg arrived, Alice had only a few days to live.

The journey back home to Murrells Inlet was not an easy one. The weather was bad, plus there were several rivers to cross by ferry. Several times the carriage got stuck in the sand and mud, forcing the ailing teenager to spend agonizing hours stranded in the storm.

At last they pulled up in front of the oaks surrounding The Hermitage, and Alice was taken upstairs to her bedroom. Something sparkling around his sister's neck caught Dr. Flagg's attention. When he noticed the ring, he slipped it off while she slept and threw it into the marshes.

Sometime during the night Alice awoke and noticed her ring missing. She jumped out of bed and ran around the house crying, "I want my ring. Give me my ring."

To calm her down, Dr. Allard took his own ring and put it on her hand. To this, Alice is said to have retorted: "I don't want your ring, Allard. Keep your own ring. I shall find mine in death."

Alice never saw her own ring again—at least in life. She died sometime during the night. When family members found her the next morning, her pillow was wet with tears.

Alice was dressed in her favorite white gown and buried in the front yard of her plantation home. A short time later, her remains were dug up and moved to the graveyard of a nearby Episcopal church. The family marked her grave with a plain marble stone, but Alice's engagement had disgraced them so much her slab was denied the dignity of the family name.

The only word etched on the stone is "Alice."

Today, visitors to the moss-shrouded cemetery often comment on the eerie silence and drifting shadows. Some say that if you walk around the grave thirteen times, Alice's ghost will appear.

Until his death a few years ago, Clarke Wilcox, an old-timer whose family bought The Hermitage in 1910, used to entertain visitors by telling them stories about Alice's ghost. Part of his performance was to lead guests upstairs to Alice's bedroom, which is virtually unchanged, even after all these years.

The same furniture is there, so is the view from the gabled window of the marshy grasses and shallow waters of the inlet facing the house. On a wall near the window is the portrait of a young girl, Alice Flagg, on her sixteenth birthday. It has been described as "one of the most beautiful faces that was ever put on canvas."

Even with bright sunlight streaming through the window, the immediate impression one receives upon entering that room is that he is not alone.

"Sometimes I can't tell her presence at all," Wilcox once confided to a reporter. "But at other times I know she's there."

Wilcox said a lot of visitors—"especially young ones"—don't like to sign the guest register at The Hermitage for fear Alice's ghost will track them down.

Many times Alice has been seen entering the front door and moving silently up the staircase to the bedroom that belonged to her. One visitor said he saw a "ghostly young woman clad in a burial gown" wandering the salt-marshes near her home.

Another visitor arriving by automobile once told Wilcox that he had passed a lovely young girl on the way up the circular driveway. The girl was dressed in white, the visitor said, but when he stopped to talk to her she disappeared.

"Oh, that was just Alice," the old man cracked. "Happens all the time. She was just out looking for her ring."

❖

AMITYVILLE HORROR

Were demonic voices behind mass murder?

The horror began on a cold November morning in 1974 when demonic voices supposedly commanded 22-year-old Ronald DeFeo to pick up his high-powered rifle and slaughter his parents and four brothers and sisters while they slept in their beds.

At his trial DeFeo claimed it was these demonic voices—not drugs or hatred for his father as reported by the newspapers—that drove him to murder his entire family. He was sentenced to six consecutive 25 year-to-life prison terms.

The horrifying incident was fairly forgotten until the following summer when George and Kathy Lutz moved into the handsome Dutch Colonial at 112 Ocean Avenue, an upscale residential section of Amityville on Long Island.

The Lutzes had known about the murders but decided the neighborhood would be the perfect place to raise their three children. Less than a month later they would be gone, however, chased away by a series of paranormal events that turned their "dream home" into the most famous haunted residence in the world.

A book by Jay Anson two years later detailed the Lutz's brief but horrifying ordeal. Ghostly voices, oozing slime, blood-splattered walls, levitating pigs, glowing red eyes, infestations of flies and a pit into hell in the basement were just some of the spectral happenings revealed in *The Amityville Horror*, which became the basis for a hit movie staring James Brolin and Margot Kidder.

Other phenomena included black slime bubbling from toilets, hooded specters parading about the house, cold spots, an attack of killer flies, the sound of an invisible brass band in the living room, doors slamming and green slime pouring out of the walls. An invisible voice spoke to one of the daughters, and cloven hoof tracks were discovered in the back yard.

At one point, unseen voices urged the Lutzes to "get out" of the house. The same diabolical presence woke them up every night at the exact same time—3:15 a.m.—that the murders took place. George Lutz grew a beard and started acting strangely. Family members commented on how he was beginning to look like the photos they had seen of Ronald DeFeo.

The Lutzes tried everything to battle the evil within their house. They prayed, sang, even tried to reason with the diabolical forces arrayed against them. A priest was called in to exorcise the place, but fled before the ritual was completed. Psychic investigators and other religious leaders were brought in to help purge their home of the "unclean spirits" tormenting their lives.

In the end, after ten days of battling the horror, they gave up and fled, leaving their belongings behind.

It should be noted that two of New England's most respected clairvoyants—Ed and Lorraine Warren of the New England Society for Psychic Research—had spent time in the house working with the Lutzes to understand what it was they were up against. The Warrens found "strong evidence" that the property was either haunted or possessed by malevolent spirits.

One report revealed that the house was located on the site of an ancient Indian ceremonial center where blood-lettings were commonly held to appease evil spirits. Another study showed that a sorcerer named John Ketcham had settled on the spot after fleeing Massachussetts in the late 1600s on charges of practicing witchcraft.

While news about the Amityville house continued to make headlines around the world, a few skeptics stepped forward to say the whole thing was a hoax perpetrated by the Lutz family and their lawyer, William Weber, who had also represented Ronald DeFeo.

"Their primary objective was to make money on a book and movie deal," said Dr. Steven Kaplan, president of the Parapsychology Society of Long Island.

Kaplan and others argued that George and Kathy Lutz dreamed up the story after moving in with relatives because they "felt creepy" at the Amityville house. Kaplan maintained he had photographs and tapes to show it was a hoax but never produced the material, even when offered $5,000 by the Warrens.

Charges by Kaplan and other skeptics have been disputed by several investigators who support the Lutz family's story. The Warrens, for example, found that Lutze's description of the paranormal activity in the home were very accurate for a case of demonic possession—even though the Lutzes had never studied demonology and would not have known how to fabricate the story they told.

The story came close to unraveling when Weber, the attorney who had represented DeFeo, sued the Lutzes for stealing his ideas for the Amityville horror. That case was settled out of court, along with others brought by subsequent occupants of the house who complained about all the negative publicity and non-stop tourists.

But many questions remained. Some investigators wanted to know how it was possible that a high-powered rifle could be fired at least six times in the dead of a winter night without arousing neighbors. Why were all of the murder victims found in identical positions—facedown in their beds with their hands crossed under their heads?

Killer DeFeo changed his story several times at trial. At first he said he killed his family while under the influence of drugs. He later changed that story, saying he had hated his father and had been plotting to kill him for months. Finally, he said "voices" commanded him to do the deed, and that "shadow ghosts" accompanied him as he went from room to room, slaying each family member.

Noteworthy is the fact that a string of bizarre coincidences occurred to people involved with the Amityville story. Actor James Brolin, who played George Lutz, was injured in a minor accident on the set. Author Jay Anson, who never actually visited the house he wrote about, suffered a heart attack while completing the last chapter of the book. He recovered, but had a second, fatal heart attack while writing his second book, *666*, about the anti-Christ.

Was the Amityville horror real? Or was the whole thing a carefully concocted get-rich scheme by the Lutzes? Almost three decades later, investigators still debate the answer to what many considered the most famous haunting in American history.

After their dramatic flight from the house, the Lutzes

moved to California where they continued to write books and articles about their experience at Amityville. Ironically, subsequent owners of "High Hopes," the original name of the house, dismissed notions that the place was ever haunted. Claiming they had "suffered inordinately" when the story went public, owners Jim and Barbara Cromarty even sued the Lutzes and won.

Judge Jack Weinstein, who presided over one of the many libel cases concerned with the Amityville story, said, "The evidence shows fairly clearly that the Lutzes, during this entire period, were considering and acting with the thought of having a book published."

After studying the case for months, Dr. Kaplan concluded: "We found no evidence to support any claim of a haunted house... What we did find is a couple who had purchased a house that they economically could not afford. It is our professional opinion that the story of its haunting is mostly fiction."

The real Amityville house still stands, but the number of its address has been changed. New siding and windows to replace the sinister looking panes at the top of the house—where the glowing red eyes were often seen—have helped the current owners disguise the exterior.

Visitors still find the handsome old Dutch Colonial anyway, drawn by an insatiable curiosity to see the most famous haunted house in America.

❖

BARNSLEY GARDENS

Old Indian curse tormented young planter

Eighteen-year-old Godfrey Barnsley arrived in America in 1823 with a dream -- to make a fortune in the cotton trade and marry a beautiful woman who would give him lots of children.

He also aspired to build a big house--not an ordinary plantation, but a grand, Mediterranean-style villa with stucco walls and soaring towers surrounded by springs, exotic gardens and marble statuary from around the world. Alas, with a lackluster education and only the ragged clothes on his back, how could this penniless lad from Liverpool possibly hope to accomplish such lofty goals?

Guided by sheer determination and an unwavering sense of destiny, Barnsley quickly set out to make his dreams come true. He worked hard as a brokerage clerk to a prominent cotton shipper and rose swiftly in both business and social worlds. Along the way he married Julia Scarborough, a beautiful young Savannah socialite and daughter of one of wealthiest and most powerful men in the South, William Scarborough II.

By his twenty-fifth birthday, Godfrey Barnsley seemed to have it all—wealth, a beautiful wife and eight handsome children. He had amassed a fortune, with a fleet of ships and offices in Savannah, New York, New Orleans and back home in Liverpool. The only thing left to do was build the grand house of his dreams—a task he began in 1841 after a sight-seeing trip by wagon train to remote Bartow County in the far north Georgia mountains.

On a whim, the prosperous young businessman purchased 3600 acres of virgin timberland interlaced with rushing streams and gently rolling hills. Here, on lands once sacred to Cherokee Indians, he would build that grand house and adorn the estate with elegant gardens, imported statuary and an English-style deer park. Then he would give it all to his beloved wife as a gift.

Like other Savannahians, Barnsley felt the Georgia mountains were healthier than the coast. He also hoped the fresh air and relaxed lifestyle would rejuvenate Julia who for years had suffered from various ailments.

Barnsley envisioned a sprawling, multi-level manor with at least twenty spacious rooms and featuring hot and cold running water--unheard of conveniences for that time. Tiles for the veranda would be imported from Spain. Doors and paneling would be fashioned by British cabinetmakers and mantels of black-and-white marble would be shipped in from Italy.

There would be boxwood gardens, fish pools and flowing fountains, croquet grounds and gardens of rare roses. Barnsley would spare no expense in creating for Julia one of the most fashionable and desirable estates in the world, a veritable paradise in the high country of north Georgia.

Everything went according to plan at first. The Barnsley's arrived in 1841 and settled into a temporary log cabin while construction on the main house began. They planted gardens, built playgrounds and dug fishponds. Gradually, the estate--which they now called The Woodlands--grew to encompass more than 10,000 acres.

Three years later tragedy struck. While visiting her doctor in Savannah, Julia took a turn for the worse and died. Devastated, Barnsley withdrew to The Woodlands where he continued work on the mansion, the gift Julia would never see. He built a library, billiards room, two drawing rooms, reception hall and separate quarters for housekeepers and grounds-men. He stuffed the house with expensive furniture and his priceless collection of paintings and other art objects.

Nothing, it seemed, could ease his remorse. Without Julia, the great house felt cold and empty. Each day after the workers left, he would wander the gardens, weeping and calling out his dead wife's name. He sought desperately to establish contact, to communicate with his wife's spirit.

Visitors to The Woodlands often saw him talking and gesturing as if to an unseen presence. On many occasions passersby spotted the wispy form of a young woman gliding through the gardens or wandering across the acorn-shaped hill on which the mansion stood. Some caught glimpses of a young woman's forlorn face peering from tower windows. Those who had known Julia swore the apparition bore a striking resemblance to the dead woman.

Sadly, Julia's death was only the first in a long string of misfortunes that would plague Barnsley for the rest of his life. Freakish accidents claimed the lives of several of his children, while the collapse of the Southern economy following the Civil War laid waste to his estate and ruined him financially.

Some say the trouble was linked to an old Indian curse. According to legend, a Cherokee chief cursed the ground because the federal government had uprooted his people in the 1830s and sent them marching westward. No white man would ever know peace on the ground, which the Cherokee claimed was sacred.

Nobody thought much about the curse until Julia's death. The string of tragic mishaps that followed forced many to conclude there might have been something to the old curse after all.

Not long after Julia's death, Barnsley's youngest son died in a freak accident. In the autumn of 1858 his teenage daughter died in the house. That same year, another son was killed by Chinese pirates while in the Orient searching for exotic plants for the estate's formal gardens. In Savannah, a son-in-law was crushed to death while overseeing a transfer of logs.

By then the unfortunate planter was beside himself with grief and worry. He blamed his misfortune on the curse, and sought out mediums, psychics and religious leaders to help undo what the old Indian chief had done to him long ago.

Barnsley's plight did not end with the sad demise of family members. Beginning in late 1860, one business venture after another failed. Barnsley's once sizeable fortune had soon been reduced to a pathetic fraction of its former worth. A few months later, with the outbreak of war, the miserable planter was left alone with his unfinished manor house and a ruined cotton-buying operation.

Barnsley's once handsome estate now lay in shambles, along with his dream of becoming one of the most prosperous planters in the South. Where roses and wisteria once blossomed on sun-splashed verandas, thick vines and weeds now twisted and crept. In time, nothing but shadows stirred among the cracked walls and crumbling walkways.

On his deathbed, Barnsley reportedly begged a minister to rid his property of its evil curse. It was too late to bring back his family, of course, or to restore his health and fortune, but at least he hoped future owners would be spared misfortune and grief.

Years after Barnsley's death, a tornado swirled in from the north, blowing off the mansion's roof and scattering his exotic plantings to the four winds. Unable to rebuild or even keep up the grounds, descendents simply let the old estate fall to ruin.

In the summer of 1989, almost 150 years after Barnsley set out to establish his cotton empire in the foothills of Georgia, another Cherokee returned to the estate to undo the old chief's curse. Richard Bird, a medicine man from Cherokee, North Carolina, said he knew something was wrong the moment he stepped onto the property.

"There was definitely something here when we got here…there was something," he told reporters. "I had a funny feeling inside…I can't explain it. It was kind of a nervousness, like butterflies in my stomach, like a cold sweat."

Bird was hired to perform a "casting out' ceremony by an attorney representing the estate's new owner, a German prince who in recent years has converted Barnsley Gardens into a luxurious golf resort. The ceremony must have worked, because the estate has apparently been free of trouble ever since.

Old stories linger, however, about ghosts and curses and Godfrey Barnsley's tragic fate. Visitors to these haunted grounds often wonder how things might have turned out for the handsome young Englishman had he heeded the old chief's wisdom and built his wife a mansion elsewhere--anywhere but that accursed, acorn-shaped hill.

BELL WITCH

Angry spirit drove Tennessee farmer to his grave

When John Bell first heard the horrible scratching sound at the walls of his remote Tennessee homestead, he thought it was rats trying to gnaw their way in out of the winter cold.

Several nights in a row he had set traps. Nothing seemed to work against the pesky rodents. Each night it was the same—scratching and clawing and hissing, keeping his family up until the wee hours. The strange thing was, no matter how hard he looked, he never saw the first sign of a rat.

Then came a new sound—tapping at the window. Before the family had time to adjust to the new disturbance, however, there were more strange noises—mysterious thumping sounds at the door, like a wild animal trying to get in. Most chilling were the eerie cries that seemed to float down the chimney long after the fire had gone out at night.

John Bell was not a superstitious fellow. All his life he had believed there was an answer to every mystery, no matter how crazy or puzzling. That's why it took took him so long to come to the conclusion that the strange noises were being made by a ghost or spirit or some such supernatural thing.

In those days, back in the early 1800s, much of Tennessee was wild and remote, full of old stories and legends about "spirits of the earth." These spirits were said to be mostly benign—actually helpful to hard-working pioneers of the lonely forests and mountains.

But, occasionally, tales cropped up about less friendly entities—malign spirits that sought to harm and destroy rather than help and instruct. Frightening stories had been left behind by the earliest explorers in the region—and the Indians before them—about dark forces in the forest that seemed to work outside the framework of normal Christian thinking.

Ironically, the Bell household seemed hardly suited for such a haunting. Handsome, prosperous and blessed with a beautiful wife and eight healthy children, the Tennessee planter hob-knobbed with the rich and famous, including nearby neighbor Andrew Jackson, the hero of New Orleans and future president of the United States.

All that changed that cold winter in 1817 when the Bell plantation became center stage for one of the most terrifying hauntings in American history.

According to legend, the whole thing started when Bell shot at a black, dog-like creature while hunting in the snowy woods near his Adams, Tennessee, home. A few hours later, a huge black bird with "fiery red eyes" attacked his daughter in the front yard.

The Bells thought nothing more about the weird occurrences until that night when they heard strange knocking and rapping noises on the outside doors and windows. Two of the Bell boys were awakened by scary hissing and gnawing sounds coming from the ceiling. They said it sounded like "giant rats trying to gnaw their way through the roof."

Bell became convinced his home was beset with demons and called in a priest. On his way to the Bell farm, so the story goes, the priest's wagon got stuck in mud and couldn't be moved. Resuming his journey on foot, the priest was eventually forced back by a "demon wind."

Friends and neighbors who visited the Bell home were shocked and frightened by the paranormal activity. Even Old Hickory, who spent the night in the house several times, came away convinced the place was cursed by some unknown evil spirit. The future president even hired a "witch layer"—a professional witch doctor—to shoot the spirit with a silver bullet.

Shortly after the witch layer's arrival, however, the spirit slapped and clawed him, finally chasing him from the house.

As news about the Bell witch haunting spread, everyone wanted to know why John Bell and his family had been singled out for such torment.

"If we didn't know them (the Bells) for the good and honest people that they were," one neighbor reported in the local newspaper, "we'd have thought they were being punished for some crime or sin they'd committed."

John Bell and his teenage daughter, Betsy, apparently bore the brunt of the witch's rage. While Bell was poked, slapped and scratched almost on an hourly basis, the entity seemed to take special pleasure in torturing Betsy each night by filling her bedroom with screams and wild laughter. By most accounts, Lucy Bell—John's wife—was rarely bothered by the capricious presence.

By the winter of 1818, life at the Bell farm had become so bizarre John Bell thought about relocating his family somewhere safe. Pictures would fall mysteriously off walls. Tables turned on their sides and scuttled across the kitchen floor. Chairs pranced about and somersaulted. Cutlery paraded up and down on the floor. China dishes and cups "marched merrily along" the tables and cabinets.

Eventually, accounts of the eerie happenings began to appear in newspapers as far away as New York and Philadelphia. Reporters, ministers, doctors and psychic researchers soon descended on the Bell household, along with hundreds of curiosity seekers. The Bell farm had become what one reporter called "a place of occult pilgrimage."

The presence of so many visitors actually seemed to encourage the spooky antics at the old Bell place. Whenever outsiders called upon the "spirit" to do something, it always obliged, sometimes making vague whispering sounds and indistinct mutterings while whipping sheets and quilts through the air and causing the clock to chime for hours at a time.

On March 14, 1818, the first distinguishable words came forth from the spirit. In the presence of several astonished visitors and the entire Bell family, a crackling woman's voice announced: "I am a spirit who was once happy... but now I have been disturbed and am unhappy."

The spirit identified herself simply as "Kate." She said she was now a witch of the forest but had once lived as a woman on the land "long, long ago." Kate informed her listeners that she was haunting the Bell farm because someone had disturbed her bones.

"My bones are buried near here," Kate said, "and I want them back."

Although John Bell succeeded in finding what he believed were the old woman's bones and providing them with a proper Christian burial, the annoying spirit refused to leave the family alone. If anything, Bell's noble action seemed to make matters worse—especially for Bell himself, who thereafter became the favorite target of the old spirit's mischievous antics.

First of all, the victimized farmer's tongue began to swell until it filled most of his mouth. He could hardly eat, speak or even swallow water. His physical condition quickly deteriorated as the old hag tormented him.

"We have seen nothing like it in our experience of morbid and pathological conditions," one attending physician declared. "There appears to be no known reason for the affliction, and there is certainly no known cure."

Bell's condition steadily worsened. Unseen hands slapped him across the face, ripped clothes from his body, punched him in the stomach. On one occasion, the witch even spat in his face.

"I'm almost done with you, Jack Bell," the witch proclaimed. "It won't be long now before you go to your grave to rot!"

Friends and neighbors begged the witch to release the farmer from her wrath. "Why do you hate John Bell so?" a friend, Jack Johnson, asked. "What has he ever done to harm or pester you?"

To this, the witch replied: "I am a spirit from everywhere—from heaven, hell and the earth. I am in the air, in houses, anyplace at any time. I was born millions of years ago. That's all I have to say."

Another friend, a big, strapping farmer, offered to crush the witch in a death grip. When he arrived at the house to deal with her, however, the unseen spirit cursed him and struck him several times on the face and head.

The witch continued to plague Bell and family members, striking them with boils, colds, fever and the like. Finally, on the morning of December 19, 1820, the farmer went into a stupor. His doctor said, "I can find nothing fatally wrong with him. Yet, he is most assuredly dying."

The next day, the doctor's words came true. John Bell's frail, tormented body was laid to rest in a tiny cemetery not far from the house where he had suffered for almost four years. At the funeral, the voice of the Bell witch was heard one last time, cackling and croaking triumphantly over the farmer's death.

Modern psychic investigators and journalists consider the Bell witch haunting one of the most terrifying episodes in the history of the paranormal. Some theorized that the spirit belonged to a woman named Kate Batts, a wealthy widow with whom John Bell was once engaged to marry. When the jilted woman died under mysterious circumstances, it was rumored that her ghost returned to torment her former suitor.

Another version of the story holds that Kate Batts had actually been a slave trader who was angry with John Bell over a business deal gone bad. When she died, her spirit returned from the grave to wreck vengeance on the Bell family.

The phantom witch, who sometimes called herself "Old Kate," continued to appear every few years, making predictions and frightening locals. In 1980, an owner of part of what used to be the Bell farm claimed to have seen apparitions of a dark-haired woman floating across the fields. He also said he heard mysterious knocking sounds at his door.

Not far from the old Bell farm is a cave where some say the witch fled after John Bell's death. Called the Bell

Witch Cave, some say it is still haunted by "Old Kate."
Visitors say they have seen strange figures roaming the
wooded paths near the cave and have heard knocking
sounds coming from deep within.

BERKELEY SQUARE HAUNTING

Madness plagued ghostly London mansion

For more than six decades, the old house has stood quietly in one of London's busiest shopping districts. Few of the thousands of shoppers and pedestrians who pass it daily know that the quaint structure was at one time considered to be the most dangerous haunted house in England.

Built in the late eighteenth century, 50 Berkeley Square has been the scene of numerous supernatural occurrences. Rattling chains, rapping noises, eerie blue lights, unearthly screams and the ghostly form of a young woman said to have committed suicide in the house have been reported by reliable witnesses.

Even Prime Minister George Canning, who lived there until his death in 1827, claimed to have heard strange noises and experienced other psychic phenomena in the building.

But it wasn't until the mid-Victorian era that 50 Berkeley Square earned its dubious reputation. That was when a man named Myers, a bachelor who had been jilted by his beautiful fiancée, went mad and allowed the handsome, multi-story structure to fall into disrepair.

The story goes that Myers, who acquired the house in 1859, became a bitter recluse and took to living in a small room in the garret. He never went outside and wouldn't answer the door except to receive food and water from his manservant.

One version of the story says Myers often wandered the house late at night, candle in hand, weeping and calling out fiancée's name.

Stories soon spread that the house was haunted. The magazine *Mayfair* described the house's "ghostly feeling" and claimed it "always seems oppressed into dullness by a sense of its own secret grandeur."

But the house's evil reputation preceded Myers by many years. In the 1830s, a maid went mad with fright in her room. One magazine said the maid was "found standing in the middle of her room, rigid as a corpse, with hideously glaring eyes, unable to speak."

She supposedly died the next day in an insane asylum.

The family refused to go into the maid's room. When a visitor arrived, however, he scoffed at the story and volunteered to sleep in the "haunted quarters." Later that night, the family heard him screaming and rushed in to find him dead.

"Frightened to death," read the coroner's report.

The most chilling story of all concerns two sailors from the frigate *HMS Penelope* who came to town on December 24, 1887. They found a "to let" sign on the house, but it was empty, so they let themselves in and went to sleep in a second-story bedroom.

In the middle of the night, footsteps were heard in the corridor outside the room, and a dark and shapeless "thing" (later described as a white-faced man with a gaping mouth) entered and attacked them.

One sailor escaped. The second was found impaled on the railings of the basement steps as though he had fallen through the bedroom window.

During the 1870s and 1880s, neighbors complained that the house was the source of loud noises, cries, moans and poltergeist phenomena, such as ringing bells, furniture moving about, objects, stones and books being tossed outside and windows being thrown open.

In the mid-1930s, the house was leased by the Maggs Brothers, who converted the lower level into an antiquarian bookshop. No phenomena have been reported in recent years, though many locals insist the place is still haunted.

THE BLACK SPOT

Statesman had chilling premonition of Civil War

———————

The road toward civil war between North and South was long and painful, with good men on both sides sincerely convinced of the rightness of their cause. One such man was John C. Calhoun, the ex-vice-president and fiery senator from South Carolina whose impassioned stand on states' rights, slavery and nullification earned him a reputation as the South's leading intellectual architect of secession.

Although he went to his grave a decade before the guns sounded at Fort Sumter in the spring of 1861, Calhoun apparently had a premonition of the coming conflict.

The chilling revelation had come to the aging senator in a dream shortly before his death in 1850. Details of the dream were recounted over breakfast one morning to his longtime friend, fellow fire-eater and states' rights advocate Robert Toombs of Georgia.

Toombs knew something was wrong the moment he sat down next to his old comrade. For one thing, he had never seen the old war hawk so warn and pale. Intrigued, the Georgia senator asked if anything was wrong.

"Pshaw!" Calhoun retorted, almost as if he were embarrassed by his strange affliction. "It is nothing but a dream I had last night which makes me see now a large black spot, like an ink blotch, upon the back of my right hand."

Toombs responded: "What was your dream like? I am not very superstitious about dreams, but sometimes they have a great deal of truth in them."

Calhoun leaned back in his chair and sighed. He then began to unravel one of the strangest tales Toombs had ever heard.

"At a late hour last night," Calhoun began, "as I was sitting in my room writing, I was astonished by the entrance of a visitor, who, without a word, took a seat opposite me. The manner in which the intruder entered, so perfectly self-possessed, as though my room and all within it belonged to him, excited in me as much surprise as indignation."

Calhoun said he had watched as the intruder drew closer. Then he noticed something extremely odd.

"As I raised my head to look into his features, I discovered that he was wrapped in a thin cloak which effectively concealed his face."

In a soft tone the stranger spoke: "What are you writing, senator from South Carolina?"

Calhoun replied that he was "writing a plan for the dissolution of the American Union."

"Senator from South Carolina," the presence whispered, "will you allow me to look at your right hand?"

At that moment the figure rose and his cloak fell away. Calhoun slumped backward, terrified at what he saw.

"I saw his face," Calhoun explained. "The sight struck me like a thunderclap. It was the face of a dead man whom extraordinary events had called back to life. The features were those of George Washington, and he was dressed in a general's uniform."

As if in a dream, Calhoun extended his right hand, as

requested. He said a "strange thrill" passed through his body as the stranger grasped his hand and held it to the light.

"After holding my hand for a moment, he looked at me steadily and said in a quiet way, 'And with this right hand, senator from South Carolina, you would sign your name to a paper declaring the Union dissolved?'"

Calhoun replied that he would, "if a certain contingency arises."

At that moment, a mysterious black blotch appeared on the back of his hand. Alarmed, the senator asked: "What is that?"

The shadowy figure readjusted his hood and said no more. But from beneath the cloak he withdrew an object which he laid upon the table—the bony hand of a skeleton.

"There," whispered the phantom in a faraway voice, "are the bones of Isaac Hayne, who was hung at Charleston by the British. He gave his life in order to establish the Union."

Suddenly the stranger disappeared, along with the skeletal hand, and Calhoun awoke in his bed. Then, recalling the dream, he slowly turned his eyes toward the back of his right hand.

What he saw made him gasp.

The black spot was still there.

BORLEY RECTORY

The most haunted house in England

Borley Rectory, a gloomy, twin-gabled Victorian mansion atop a muddy hill overlooking the Stour River in England's Essex County, was once described as one of the ugliest houses in England.

Before it mysteriously burned to the ground more than sixty years ago—precisely at the stroke of midnight—some said the red-brick, Gothic monstrosity located sixty miles northeast of London was also one of the most haunted structures in the world.

For more than a century, the rambling old house—supposedly built on the grounds of an ancient monastery—was the scene of strange noises, phantom coaches that came and went at midnight, mysterious cold spots, fires and unending poltergeist activity. Locals said it was cursed as well as haunted and refused to go anywhere near the place, especially after dark.

The most commonly reported apparition was that of a young nun, said to have been buried alive on the grounds more than five centuries ago. The nun was reportedly seen at all hours of the day and night, a gray, diaphanous form gliding along a dark path dubbed "nun's walk."

Other phenomena included heavy footsteps tramping up and down stairways late at night, objects appearing and disappearing, bells ringing and mysterious writing on walls. Organ music was often heard coming from nearby Borley Church, along with weird monastic chanting.

In 1945, *The Times* of London called Borley Rectory "the most haunted house in England." Built in 1863 for the Reverend Henry Dawson Ellis Bull, the brooding old building with its dark rooms, ugly turrets and harsh red brick was supposedly situated on the site of an abandoned Benedictine monastery. Ghostly encounters began almost as soon as the rector and his family moved in.

"We heard strange footsteps almost every night," the rector wrote in his diary. "Bells rang constantly. Voices whispered to us in the dark."

One daughter was awakened by a slap in the face. Another saw the dark figure of an old man in a tall hat by her bed. One frequent visitor saw the nun's apparition several times.

No one was ever harmed, but the experiences were unnerving.

The vicar's son, Harry Bull, took over the rectory in 1892 and stayed until 1927. In that period a headless man was seen in the bushes; a phantom coach appeared almost every night; a cook reported that a locked door was open every morning; and four of the Reverend Bull's sisters together saw a young nun who disappeared in full view.

Edwin Whitehouse, who later became a Benedictine monk, visited the rectory with his aunt and uncle during 1931. On one occasion a fire started in the baseboard of an unused room. As the flames were put out, a flint the size of a hen's egg fell to the floor.

Later, while the vicar conducted a service of exorcism in his room, Edwin and his aunt were hit by falling stones.

In the fall of 1930, the Reverend Lionel A. Foyster and his wife Marianne moved in. Before they fled from the house five years later, the Foysters were bombarded with hot stones, spat at, levitated, punched and screamed at by unseen forces. Objects flew through the air, bottles smashed, fires broke out at random, keys and money went missing and articles of clothing vanished.

For some reason, Marianne Foyster's presence seemed to increase spiritual activity. On several occasions, the nun tried to contact the reverend's young wife by scrawling pleas for help on the walls.

"Marianne, please help me get out," the scrawling read.

Researchers theorized that the spectral nun had met a particularly cruel fate in the early sixteenth-century century. Old records indicate that, about 1534, a novice (a nun who has not yet taken her vows) fell in love with a young monk at the Borley monastery.

In those days, nuns and priests were required to remain celibate under pain of excommunication or death. When the couple was captured trying to flee in a coach, the authorities strangled the monk, hanged the coachman and walled up the nun alive in a basement beneath the Priory.

The ghosts of the nun, monk and hired coachmen accounted for most of the sightings at Borley. Altogether, there were more than two-thousand paranormal events at the house.

In 1937, Captain W.H. Gregson bought Borley Rectory. Fully aware of its haunted reputation, Gregson enlisted Harry Price, the flamboyant founder of Britain's National Laboratory of Psychical Research, to investigate. Price spent the next ten years probing the famous house's occult secrets, even inviting people who were "intrepid, critical and unbiased" to join his team.

Ellice Howe, an Oxford graduate who accepted Price's challenge, swore he saw objects move. Others in the group reported unexplained noises. Commander A.B. Campbell of the BBC "Brains Trust" team, was hit by a piece of soap in a sealed room. Dr. C.E.M. Joad, the famed philosopher, another member of the team, reported that a thermometer recorded a sudden and inexplicable drop of ten degrees.

Prices' investigation was sharply criticized by the media, noting that the celebrated author and parapsychologist had a reputation for showmanship and should not be taken seriously. After his death in 1948, allegations of fraud were made, but none proved.

Precisely at midnight on the night of February 27, 1939, Borley Rectory caught fire and burned. Some observers claimed they heard screams of anguish emanating from the flames, though no one was in the house at the time.

In 1943, four years after the rectory was destroyed, excavators digging a trench found fragments of a woman's skull and pendants bearing religious symbols. The woman's identity was never revealed, but some investigators suspect foul play was involved and linked her ghost to some of the supernatural manifestations at Borley Rectory.

One year later, in 1944, a *Life* magazine photographer and *Time-Life* reporter watched spellbound while a heavy brick rose more than four feet into the air over the ruins of Borley Rectory.

Strange things continued to happen on the property, even as late as 1961 when flashlights, car headlights and camera flashes all failed during an investigation of the site. In 1953 and again in 1954, newspapers reported sightings of ghosts in the vicinity of the rectory. Bricks taken from the Borley ruins and buried under a school playground at Wellingborough were connected with the alleged appearance of a ghost.

Even after all these years, Borley Rectory continues to fascinate skeptics as well as serious paranormal investigators. In 1988, one London newspaper quipped: "The haunting at the old Rectory might have been nothing more than a load of rubbish, but what fascinating rubbish it was."

THE BOY WHO SEES GHOSTS

'Shadow People' drove family from home

The horror began with a blood-curdling scream in the dead of night.

Denice Jones, a 32-year-old Manchester, Connecticut, housewife, was cleaning up the kitchen after a late dinner when she heard a "shrill keening" coming from her youngest son's bedroom upstairs. She flew up the stairs and found 8-year-old Michael curled up in a dark corner of the room, a terrified look on his face.

He told her a "crayon color white" man came into his room and tried to touch his shoulder.

"He said he was my dead grandfather and was trying to warn me to stay away from the other bad ghosts," the boy told his mother.

It wasn't the first time that a ghostly presence had bothered the boy—nor would it be the last. For more than a year, Michael and other family members had been plagued by sightings of ghosts, demons, glowing balls of light, levitating furniture and—most frightening of all—red-eyed apparitions with blood-stained teeth that kept trying to bite Michael.

Denice Jones, who had gone through a painful divorce before recently marrying Bruce Jones, said most of the turmoil centered around Michael. Particularly disturbing was the dark image of a faceless man that kept appearing in Michael's room as well as the bloodied head of another specter.

"It has been hell, very scary," Denice said during interviews on *Prime Time Live, Inside Edition, CNN* and other network television shows.

The incident became the basis for a new book, *The Other Side: The True Story of the Boy Who Sees Ghosts* (New Horizon Press).

The strange events started in the fall of 1998, shortly after Bruce and Denice moved into an old, Colonial-style house in Manchester with their three children—Kenny, Michael and Crystal. At first they tried to downplay the odd occurrences, thinking they were pranks, hallucinations or their imagination.

But things got worse—much worse.

"We'd be sitting on the couch and it would lift a foot or so off the floor and slam down," Denice told *The New York Post*.

Several times family members were "slapped" by invisible hands and had their hair or clothes yanked by some unseen presence. Blankets and sheets would fly off beds at random while plates, glasses and silverware flew through the air. Toys were constantly being pulled off shelves and broken, and clothes were snatched from closets and drawers and ripped apart.

One day Michael found an old photograph in a trunk. It was his grandfather, who had died long before the boy was born.

"That's the man who keeps coming into my room at night to warn me," Michael told his mother.

When scratch and bite marks started appearing on Michael's body, Denice decided enough was enough. She took her son to counselors, psychiatrists and other medical specialists for answers. They even called in church groups to bless the house. One group ran screaming from the house claiming it was "full of devils."

Finally, they found a defrocked Catholic priest who agreed to exorcise the house of demons.

The Reverend Roy F. McKenna, head of Our Lady of the Rosary Chapel in Monroe, Connecticut, was no stranger to exorcism—or controversy. Since the 1960s, the 70-year-old priest had performed dozens of exorcisms without approval of the Church.

When he refused to stop the practice after several warnings, Monsignor Thomas Ginty, chancellor of the Archdiocese of Hartford, said Reverend McKenna was officially ostracized from the Roman Catholic Church.

"He was exactly what we were looking for," Denice noted. "Everybody else turned us down or were unable to help us."

Unable to free themselves from the growing danger, the Jones family moved to another house. That didn't stop the haunting, though.

"They followed us everywhere we went," she said.

Today, Denice Jones and her family live in Deerfield Beach, Florida, where Michael continues to see ghosts. The specters don't appear to be as threatening, but the Jones family still finds sharing a home with ghosts uncomfortable.

DEVIL BABY

Cursed mother gave birth to abomination

In the winter of 1913, all of Chicago was talking about the so-called "devil baby" that supposedly lived at Hull House, the controversial immigrant settlement center founded more than two decades earlier by famed social crusader Jane Addams.

According to one report circulating among the poorer wards of the city, the thing—whatever it was—had horns, cloven feet, pointed ears, a tail and scaly skin.

"It looks like Satan himself," one terrified woman told a newspaper reporter.

Other witnesses claimed the strange infant could talk, walk and fly about the house at will. Until it was locked up in the attic, the abomination regularly mocked God and cursed priests who offered to baptize it.

No one really knows where the baby came from or how the story got started. There are several versions, but the most popular one involved a young Italian girl named Rose who defied her family and married an atheist.

A few months after their wedding, so goes the story, the new bride hung a picture of the Virgin Mary on the wall. This angered her husband, who tore it down, ripped it up and swore he would rather have the Devil in the house. The couple was punished with the birth of a baby that looked like a miniature Satan. A few weeks after its birth, the father bundled the monster up and took it to Hull House.

Although Jane Addams denied the story to the end, legend has it that she took the child in, then quickly locked it away in an upper room where it remained until its death in the 1930s.

Word spread quickly. Visitors, some from as far away as New York and California, flocked to Hull House for a glimpse of the amazing spawn. The small staff was besieged with countless letters and telephone calls inquiring about the Devil Baby.

Hull House, built in 1856 by Chicago millionaire Charles J. Hull, was purchased by Jane Addams in the late 1880s. With friend Ellen Starr, Addams transformed the rambling old mansion into a haven for the city's large influx of immigrants, many of them desperately poor and in need of food, shelter and education.

For years, this section of Chicago was one of the most fashionable. Things changed, however, following the Great Fire of 1871 when wealthy residents moved out. Large numbers of immigrants—especially Greek, Italian and Jewish settlers—poured into the area, turning it into the "darkest corner" of Chicago.

Prostitution and drugs were rampant. Exiled criminals from other parts of the city found refuge among the grimy streets and run-down tenement houses where crooked cops oversaw illegal saloons, bordellos and gambling houses. All in all, it was a horrible place to live—especially for the ever-growing numbers of poor ethnic groups who swarmed into the neighborhood in search of jobs and shelter.

It was only natural that tales about ghosts, "devil babies" and other old beliefs would take root and flourish in the new environment.

What caused such a bizarre story to gain credence in

the ethnic neighborhoods of Chicago? According to Beth Scott and Michael Norman, authors of *Haunted Heartland*, the "gossipy tongues of immigrant women" were mainly responsible.

"Surrounded as they were by a foreign culture, these women clung tenaciously to the ways of the Old World," they wrote. "Miracles, curses and the supernatural were considered possible in the cultures they brought with them to America."

The existence of the "devil baby," for example, seemed perfectly normal to these women whose family, home, religion, traditions and superstitions were the cornerstone of their lives.

"If a woman questioned the teachings of her elders, dared to marry outside her religion or station in life, or in any way disrupted the pattern of behavior expected of her, the penalties were harsh," the authors explained.

The "devil baby" was simply God's way of punishing those who strayed from the fold, theorized researcher Rosemary Ellen Guiley.

"The story seemed to fit well with the moral traditions of the time," she said. "You break God's law, the devil's going to come get you."

Jane Addams seemed to understand what motivated these women. She wrote of the "devil baby" uproar: "It was the old women who really seemed to have come into their own, and perhaps the most significant result of the incident was the reaction of the story upon them. It stirred their minds and memory as with a magic touch, it loosened their tongues and revealed the inner life and thoughts of those who are so often inarticulate…"

The story refuses to die. Even today, people occasionally claim to catch a glimpse of the little monster leering at them from an upper-level window of Hull House.

Hull House is regarded as one of Chicago's most haunted houses and is regularly included in "haunted tours" of the city. Besides the "devil baby," numerous ghosts supposedly haunt the house, including those of Mrs. Charles Hull and Jane Addams herself.

During an overnight stay in the 1920s, Helen Campbell, author of *Prisoners of Poverty*, said she saw an apparition hovering over her bed. She described the figure as a sad-faced old woman who apparently meant no harm. When she lit a candle, however, the gloomy phantom vanished.

In her book, *Twenty Years at Hull House*, Jane Addams confessed that prior occupants of the house often heard strange footsteps and moaning sounds on the second floor. Some placed buckets of water on the stairs, thinking the ghost or ghosts would be unable to cross it.

DIALING THE DEAD

Phone calls from beyond the grave

Just past midnight on October 21, 1944, Ida Lupino was awakened by the sound of the telephone ringing. The Hollywood actress was accustomed to late-night phone calls, but this time, as she hurried to the phone, a strange sensation came over her.

"It was as if I was floating in a cloud over a big, blue ocean, all shining and vast," she explained.

When she picked up the receiver and heard her father's voice on the other end, she almost fainted. That's because Stanley Lupino had been killed six months earlier in London during a German air raid.

"But it was my father I heard on the other line," Lupino emphasized. "The voice was scratchy and seemed to come from far away, but I'd know it anywhere."

In his usual cheery voice, the "dead" man proceeded to relate information concerning his estate. He specifically told his daughter where to find certain stock certificates and other documents that had been missing since his death.

Lupino's strange phone call was not unique. Since the advent of the telephone, hundreds of people claim to have received similar phone calls from the dead, including Thomas Alva Edison, who believed that electric wires could connect the living with the dead.

According to researchers of the paranormal, most calls come from recently departed relatives eager to impart information or to warn loved ones of impending danger. Those who receive such calls say the voices sound the same as when the deceased was living.

Also, the voices often uses pet names and words known only to the two holding the conversation. Such was the case with Ida Lupino, who believed for the rest of her life that she had received a phone call from her dead father.

According to author-researcher Rosemary Ellen Guiley, the telephone "usually rings normally, although some recipients say that the ring sounded flat and abnormal. In many cases, the connection is bad, with a great deal of static and line noise, and occasionally, the faint voices of other persons are heard, as though lines have been crossed."

Some experts say that phantom phone calls occur when the recipient is in a passive state of mind.

"If the recipient knows the caller is dead, the shock is great and the phone call very brief," noted Susy Smith, author of *The Power of the Mind.* "Invariably, the caller terminates the call after a few seconds or minutes, or the line goes dead."

Several theories exist as to the origin of phantom phone calls. Some researchers believe the calls are, indeed, placed by the dead, who somehow manipulate the telephone mechanisms and circuitry. Others said the calls are "deceptions of elemental-type spirits who enjoy playing tricks on the living."

One investigator suggested the calls are psychokinetic acts caused by the recipient, whose intense desire to communicate with the dead creates a type of hallucinatory experience, while another dismisses such phenomena outright, saying they are nothing more than a fantasy created by the recipient.

For the most part, phantom phone calls are not seriously regarded by parapsychologists. During the 1940s, however, "psychic telephones" were all the rage. Interest in the phenomenon waned until the 1960s, when some researchers theorized that ghostly voices could be captured on electromagnetic tape.

Some researchers believe it is only a matter of time before home computer operators start receiving emails from the dead.

EBO LANDING

Africans chose death over slavery on Georgia island

Sometimes late at night, when the moon is full and the wind is just right, residents along Dunbar Creek, a tributary of the Frederica River on St. Simons Island, Georgia, say they can hear a mournful chant and the ghostly clanging of iron chains.

Some say the ruckus is made by the spirits of Africans who decided to drown themselves almost two centuries ago off the Georgia coast rather than submit to slavery on a Southern plantation.

The mass suicide supposedly occurred one night in May 1803 after a boatload of slaves arrived at St. Simons for a brief stopover on its way to a South Carolina cotton plantation. While the guards slept, the chained slaves gathered themselves, jumped overboard and drowned in the swift tidal creek.

"That story has been around a long time," said the late Albert "Bo" Fendig, a retired attorney and local historian who lived on Dunbar Creek for several years. "A lot of people swear they've heard the ghosts."

It usually happens around midnight, Fendig said.

"You have to listen close. It's like a low humming sound at first, then it gets louder, and you can hear what sounds like metal chains grinding and clanking under the water."

One longtime islander said he has been awakened

many times by the sound of clanking chains and low, chanting noises coming from the place now known as Ebo Landing.

"It's eerie, all right," said Sam Davis, who worked for a while as a shrimp fisherman. "Everybody I know has heard that {weird} noise at one time or another."

According to one version, the doomed slaves came from the region of Ebo, or Ibo, a region along the coast of West Africa. The term Igbo refers to persons from the region known historically as Igboland, now Nigeria. Although Europeans and Americans spelled it Ebo, or Ibo, the Africans called themselves Igbo.

Several hundred men, women and children were rounded up in a raid and sold to European slave traders. Some of those captured had been promised freedom once they reached America.

The long voyage across the Atlantic ended when a fierce storm forced the Charleston-bound ship to seek shelter at St. Simons, a sleepy barrier island near the port city of Brunswick. While there, the shackled slaves somehow learned of the fate awaiting them.

"A great sadness came over them," goes the story. "They knew that in slavery they would no longer exist as human beings. Families would be split up, perhaps never to see one another again."

That night, under the light of a full moon, they prayed to their god, Chukwu, for an answer to their dilemma. Sometime around midnight a tall chieftain stood up and told the others he had a plan. Rather than spend the rest of their lives in bondage, they would all follow him into the creek, where they could enter paradise together.

Happiness and freedom awaited them in the world

beyond time, the chief told them. After long weeks of being cramped aboard a disease-ridden slave ship, with a bleak future awaiting them in the Carolina cotton fields, the idea sounded appealing.

The hundred or so men, women and children were instructed to wait until the moon was high. Then, when the signal was given, they said a prayer, picked up their shackles and jumped overboard.

Another version says they climbed over the side and waded into the water, chanting, "The sea brought me, and the sea will bring me home."

Most drowned, but some survived and were taken to two nearby plantations on St. Simons and Sapelo where they recovered. Over the years, the grim story was recounted in detail, gradually becoming the basis for a well-known local legend about Ebo spirits still roaming the tranquil banks of Dunbar Creek.

The legend is one of the most popular along Georgia's Golden Isles. Each year, ghost hunters come to St. Simons hopeful of touring the haunted spot where the tribesmen drowned. Ebo Landing, however, is now on private property, but can be seen from a distance when traveling east on Sea Island Road.

"A lot of people want to visit the spot," said one former chamber of commerce spokesperson. "They're usually disappointed when we tell them it's on private land. But, if they're lucky and in the right place, they can sometimes hear the chains rattling along the bottom of the creek where those poor souls drowned and entered paradise."

FLYING DUTCHMAN

Cursed captain dooms ship to sail forever

Just past midnight on January 26, 1927, British sailors rounding Cape Town, South Africa, aboard the *Carnervon* saw what appeared to be a strange light floating toward them through thick fog.

Fourth Officer N.K. Stone was quickly summoned on deck and handed the ship's telescope. What he saw made his blood run cold.

"It was an old-fashioned sailing rig, like no other I've ever seen before," he wrote in his journal. "It was green and bright and there was a luminous haze between the masts."

Five sailors, including Officer Stone, watched several minutes while the eerie apparition drifted closer. Then, all at once, it disappeared.

"I shall never forget that sight," Officer Stone recalled in an interview with Sir Ernest Bennett, a leading British investigator of the paranormal. "One minute it was here; the next it was gone. I remember telling my mates, 'my God, it's a ghost ship!'"

Until his death, the veteran seaman believed that what he saw was the fabled *Flying Dutchman*, the phantom ghost ship doomed to wander the Seven Seas forever. Countless sailors have laid claim to similar sightings over the years.

There are actually several versions to the *Flying Dutchman* legend. A German version holds that a captain named von Falkenberg gambled his soul in a dice game with the devil while sailing the North Sea. But in Britain the origin is linked to a sea captain who shook his fist at heaven and challenged God to sink his ship.

According to this version, an apparition appeared in the ship, but the captain quickly shot it. At that point the spectral visitor cursed the captain to sail forever. Misfortune would befall all who laid eyes on the doomed ship.

The most famous version of the story hails from Holland. A stubborn captain named van Stratten vowed to sail around the Cape of Storms, now known as the Cape of Good Hope. His ship sank, and all hands drowned except the captain, who had made a pact with the devil to spare his life.

Now van Stratten is captain of a ghost ship that must continue to sail the seas of the world until the end of time.

German author Heinrich Heine romanticized the *Flying Dutchman* story by writing that the doomed captain must go ashore every seven years in search of an unsullied maid. Richard Wagner adopted the story for his opera, *Die Fliegened Hollander* (*Flying Dutchman*).

The last recorded sighting was in September 1942, when four people sitting on their balcony in Cape Town saw the ghostly vessel sail into Table Bay and disappear behind Robben Island.

Efforts to follow the ship always fail, usually because of poor visibility brought on by bad weather. If a ship gets too close, however, the phantom vessel manages to disappear, often in full view of its startled crew.

GETTYSBURG GHOSTS

Phantom soldiers linger
at bloody battlefield

Late one night in October 1966, Union Civil War re-enactors camped at Gettysburg, Pennsylvania, were awakened by strange music floating through the woods. Thinking another group of re-enactors was approaching, the boys in blue got up to cheer them on and welcome them to camp.

But no one was there, only the sound of drums and fifes drawing closer in the dark.

"I tell you, a chill went down my spine as that music continued to move toward us," recalled John Rushoe, a Union re-enactor from Pennsylvania who recognized the Civil War tune. "The music seemed to be coming right out of the air."

The incident happened near Devil's Den, site of one of the bloodiest battles of the three-day Gettysburg campaign in early July 1863. Rushoe and his comrades wondered if they had experienced some kind of supernatural echo of the fighting that claimed some 51,000 casualties.

Next day, as they marched to a nearby hill called Little Round Top, the Union re-enactors were in for another spectral shock. Several said they noticed a "gray luminescent mist" possessing a vaguely human form gliding among the trees toward the hill's stony summit.

"It wasn't ground fog, I can tell you that," Rushoe explained. "The shape was over five feet tall and about a foot wide and had sort of a human shape. I'd never seen a ghost before, but I knew I was looking at one then."

The startled re-enactors watched the apparition for about a minute before it vanished.

Rushoe believes the phantom might have been the spirit of a Union solder from the 20th Maine, a regiment that courageously defended the hill. Others speculated it might have been the ghost of a Confederate soldier killed during the battle.

Rushoe and his comrades are among thousands of visitors and residents of Gettysburg who are convinced the battlefield is haunted. According to some paranormal researchers, the Civil War town and surrounding battlefield is the most haunted region in America, with a long list of ghost sightings and poltergeist activity.

By day, the picturesque town is a charming, bustling community packed with tourists, relic hunters and shoppers. Many come to see the historic buildings, battlefields, museums and solemn cemeteries that mark the fateful battle that turned the tide of war in favor of the North.

Others come to see the ghosts—the spectral remains of the thousands of soldiers, blue and gray, who perished in the fighting.

While ghostly sightings are made throughout the town, several areas appear to be particularly haunted. Devil's Den is a tangled outcropping of rocks once used by Native Americans as a burial ground. Even in the daytime it is a gloomy, unsettling place of drifting mists, shifting shadows and weird sounds.

It was here that one of the bloodiest skirmishes took

place on July 2, 1863, the second day of the battle. In 1880, Pennsylvania writer Emmanuel Bushman recounted how hundreds of people had reported "many unnatural and supernatural sights and sounds" in the Devil's Den area, including Indian war whoops and the apparitions of early settlers.

Local lore has it that the rocks mark the entrance to a bottomless cavern, a place infested with giant snakes as well as demons from the subterranean regions below. Some sources say bodies of soldiers, killed during the Civil War fighting were thrown into the pit and never recovered.

Closer to town is Pennsylvania Hall, a large, multi-columned structure located on the campus of Gettysburg College that once served as field hospital and lookout center for General Robert E. Lee. Regarded as the most haunted structure in Gettysburg, students, administrators and visitors have reported seeing shadowy sentries pacing back and forth in the Hall's cupola where Lee's staff officers were stationed.

Numerous farms and private residences have also been settings for supernatural activity. Spectral images of Confederate soldiers have been spotted at Rose Farm, once used as a field hospital and burial ground. One member of the Rose Farm family is said to have gone insane when she heard the ghostly screams of dying men on the operating table and then saw blood flowing from the walls of the house.

At the Soldier's National Museum, which served as an orphanage during the Civil War, visitors and staffers say they've heard the screams and cries of children. The wispy form of a young woman who committed suicide shortly after the war is said to wander among the woods near Spangler's Spring, a historic site south of town.

During the ferocious battle, the sound of hundreds of blasting cannon shook the ground and rattled windows. On certain nights, locals can still hear the booming roar of artillery, the crack of musketfire and the shrieks of men dying in battle—even when no re-enactors are around.

Stories are often told about "flickering orbs of blue light" hovering over battlefield and graveyards, strange music floating through trees and the mysterious way cameras and other electronic equipment malfunction for no reason.

One group of visitors saw a young soldier crying over a monument honoring a fallen Confederate general. The moment they approached, the young, gray-clad soldier vanished before their eyes.

Stories such as these have circulated for years. And, while most reports of supernatural activity are dismissed as "witness suggestibility" or outright fraud, many remain unsolved.

In 1992, for example, Stanley and Ruth Bukowski, Confederate re-enactors from northern Illinois, were at the battlefield for the filming of the movie, *Gettysburg*. They were participating in a re-creation of Pickett's Charge, the spectacular and unsuccessful attack by 15,000 Confederates on the Union lines at Cemetery Ridge.

Before they gave the Rebel Yell and charged into battle, they heard a ghostly sound from the woods behind them.

"When we heard that ghostly collective yell behind us, some of us turned around and saw that there was no one in the woods, but the sounds continued," he said.

Some investigators theorized that the gathering of several thousand re-enactors on the battlefield somehow generated a supernatural connection to Pickett's famous charge. Another re-enactor, who portrayed a Federal infantryman from the Midwest in the movie, said he was awakened in his tent one night by the sound of troops moving past.

"It was real late, about 2 a.m., I guess, and I wondered who would be stupid enough to march troops around in the dark."

The puzzled re-enactor got up to investigate—but found nothing.

Others later confirmed that they had heard similar noises. The re-enactor thinks the noise they heard was the spectral "echo" of General James Longstreet's Confederate forces marching past the exact spot more than 135 years earlier.

Some experts think it's understandable why Gettysburg is so haunted. The violent deaths of so many people in such a brief period of time, it is said, would leave their souls trapped in a kind of limbo-zone, lost and unable to adjust to their new circumstances.

That is why their specters remain, drifting and moaning in the twilight mists, never at peace as they continually answer the bugle's call to relive the bloodiest battle of the Civil War.

GHOSTLY BOARDERS

Murdered banker still occupies Selma mansion

Deep in the heart of Selma, Alabama, there stands a handsome, multi-columned mansion that has been center-stage for unexplained psychic phenomena ever since its owner was allegedly shot and killed by Yankee troops shortly after the end of the Civil War.

According to some town historians, the ghost of John Parkman still haunts the brooding old plantation home at 713 Mabry Street, which, in recent years has become one of this town's most popular tourist spots.

Parkman was a 29-year-old banker, so the story goes, who had been thrown in jail by occupying Federal forces for having illegally used bank funds to dabble in cotton speculation. He was shot while trying to escape, according to official records, even though some sources suggest he might have drowned in the Alabama River during the same escape attempt.

Whatever his mortal fate, legend has it that his ghost has been seen numerous times wandering the many rooms of Sturtivant Hall, the antebellum neoclassic mansion built in 1853. Some witnesses also claim to have seen the spirits of his two dead daughters, their young faces pressed against the window late at night and occasionally in broad daylight.

One such witness is Betty Calloway, president of the Sturtivant Museum Association. At the time of the sighting, Calloway lived across the street from the mansion.

"I saw the faces of two small girls, presumably the Parkman children, peering out an upstairs window," she said. "Another time, we called the fire department because there was smoke coming out the window of that room, but the window was closed and they found no evidence of fire or anything."

One visitor to the house, the commandant of a nearby Air Force base, also said he saw two little girls at the window. The girls were said to be staring through the glass straight onto the busy street below, as if they were anxiously awaiting someone's return.

Azile Ellis, a museum guide, said she was alone in the house one day when she heard what sounded like footsteps on the second floor.

"I was in the warming room when, all of a sudden, I could hear someone walking around upstairs. It sounded like he had stopped at the head of the stairs, so I went to the stairs and looked up. There was no one there. In fact, there was no other person in the room at that time but me."

Ellis said the footsteps turned and went into another room, where they continued for almost half an hour.

"I'm not one who goes bananas over ghosts, but there wasn't enough money to make me go up there and look," she said.

Perhaps the scariest encounter was related by Anne Davidson, a retired guide.

"One day a man came in to go through the house spraying for pests," she said. "He went upstairs, but in a few minutes he came hurriedly down. He was a newcomer to Selma, and he hadn't heard any of the stories. He said to me, 'Has anybody had any unpleasant experiences in that room at the head of the stairs?' He said someone or something had almost pushed him to the floor."

Other staff members and visitors have commented on doors opening and closing on their own, shutters flapping mysteriously and strange moaning sounds coming from the second floor.

Roy Nix, a Selma police sergeant who lived in a small house behind the plantation, also had a run-in with something strange.

"It was weird," he said. "I made rounds every night. It would be warm in a room, but suddenly it would go cold. Others have had this experience."

After Sergent Nix moved away, Troy Hughes, a medical supplies salesman, and his wife, Camille, rented the place. Ever since, they have been constantly awakened by alarm systems that go off for no reason, doors opening and closing on their own and shutters banging in the wind—even when locked from the inside.

"The only way you could open them would be from the inside of the house, and then you'd have to open the windows to get at the shutter latches," Hughes explained. "It's my responsibility to make sure the shutters are closed at night. But the shutters will be open in the morning."

One other episode convinced the Hughes that some supernatural force had invaded the home.

"One time when we were out of town, we came home and all the pictures on the wall were turned crooked," he noted. "A lot of things were moved around. The windows were sealed; there is no way anyone could have gotten in."

Hughes said they considered calling the police, but decided against it, since nothing was missing.

GHOSTS
OF FLIGHT 401
Doomed aviators warn crew from the grave

Eastern Airlines FLight 401 was making its final approach to Miami International Airport on the night of December 19, 1972, when a panel light suddenly came on, indicating trouble with the landing gear. The pilot and flight engineer went to work trying to correct the problem. In their haste, however, they failed to notice the aircraft's steady descent over the Florida Everglades until it was too late.

Seconds later, the Lockheed TriStar jumbo jet crashed, killing 98 passengers and crew members, including the pilot—Captain Bob Loft—a 30,000-hour aviator who had flown the TriStar since its introduction. Also on the flight deck were First Officer Albert Stocl and Flight Engineer Dan Repo.

An official investigation concluded that equipment failure and pilot error caused the crash. Flight recorders indicated the crew had detected a problem with the landing gear moments before its fateful plunge. In their haste to fix the problem, they did not notice the aircraft steadily losing altitude until the right wing impacted with the swamp. The ensuing crash caused the aircraft to break into pieces as it plowed into the muck.

The tragic story might have ended there had Eastern not decided to salvage parts of the downed plane and install them on other company aircraft. Soon after parts were incorporated into Flight 318, strange things started happpening.

A flight attendant making her way down the aisle of Flight 318 fainted when she saw the ghost of Captain Loft standing at the rear of the plane. Other attendants claimed to see the dead captain's reflection in windows and mirrors. One crewman said he saw the captain's ghost sitting in a passenger seat staring out the window, while another said he heard the dead captain's voice over the public address system warning passengers to put on their seatbelts.

"I knew it was the captain immediately," one frightened attendant said about the ghostly voice. Later she saw what appeared to be the dead captain standing in the aisle near the back of the plane. "He turned around and looked at me and smiled, then vanished."

Witnesses also reported experiencing abnormally cold sensations and an invisible presence aboard other L-011s that contained parts from Flight 401's wreckage. One woman complained to a stewardess that a passenger dressed in an Eastern Airlines flight officer uniform sitting next to her looked "deathly pale" and would not speak.

When the stewardess checked on the passenger, all she found was an empty seat. The startled female passenger was later shown photographs of Eastern Airlines engineers and identified Don Repo as the sick-looking man who had been sitting next to her.

On another flight, from New York to Mexico City, Repo's face appeared in the oven window, startling two stewardesses and an engineer.

"Watch out for fire on this airplane," the ghostly face

intoned in a disembodied voice.

The eerie warning almost came true while the plane sat on a Mexico City runway. Seconds before taking off, one of the plane's engines malfunctioned, and it had to turn around for repair.

There were other manifestations of supernatural activity, including tools that suddenly appeared in the hands of mechanics and power consoles that flashed on and off. Repo's uniformed ghost popped up most frequently, usually seen sitting in a plane's first class section or crew compartment. He was also seen sitting in the cockpit as well. Flight officers said Repo always seemed calm and relaxed, but "very concerned" about the safety and operation of the plane.

Whenever the dead flight engineer's ghost appeared, "It often made suggestions or gave warnings to crew members who only realized he was an apparition after he had vanished," said John Fuller, author of *The Ghost of Flight 401*.

On numerous occasions, the ghosts appeared in the cockpit where they warned crew members about equipment problems and impending danger. "But we will not let it happen," they reportedly told pilots.

The sightings—twenty in all—persisted for several months, then started tapering off after Eastern complained they were hurting business. Management threatened to fire workers who talked to the press about their ghostly experiences.

Eyewitness reports continued, however, many from high-ranking Eastern officials who had known the dead officers personally. One sighting came from a vice president of the company who allegedly spoke with a captain on a Miami-bound flight. The second he recognized the officer as Captain Loft, the apparition vanished.

In supernatural lore, ghosts frequently haunt air-planes, ships, trains, buses, carriages and other vehicles of mass transit. But paranormal investigators say the haunt-ing associated with Flight 401 was most unusual because of the large number of sightings and reluctance on the part of the specters to leave.

Fearful of adverse publicity, Eastern Airlines officials eventually stopped talking to the press—and warned employees to do likewise.

But strange stories about Flight 401 continued to cir-culate in the airline community for years. A book was eventually published detailing the crash and subsequent haunting, followed by a major motion picture starring Ernest Borgnine. An account of the paranormal happen-ings even appeared in a 1974 U.S. Flight Safety Foundation's newsletter.

GHOSTLY CHARGE

Robert E. Lee still commands
South Carolina battlefield

Does the ghost of Confederate General Robert E. Lee haunt a lonely battlefield near Aiken where outnumbered South Carolinians turned back a Union invasion during the waning days of the Civil War?

Experts are puzzled over a mysterious photograph taken in 1999 during a reenactment of the pivotal Battle of Aiken that seems to offer proof that the famous general's spirit appeared during a simulated cavalry charge.

The photo was snapped by a North Augusta photo-journalist who was on hand documenting the reenactment for the Sons of Confederate Veterans.

"It's so eerie they can't explain it," said Chris Dabrowski, an official photographer for the SCV and honorary member of the E. Porter Alexander camp.

Dabrowski said he was shooting scenes of the reenactment when he happened to notice a line of Confederate cavalrymen on a hilltop getting set to charge.

"It was on a Sunday morning in February 1999," Dabrowski recalled in an interview. "The skies were overcast and there was a slight breeze blowing in from the woods when I saw the young men on horseback at the top of the hill. One of the horses was rider-less, a tribute to a fallen comrade."

When the prints arrived a week later, Dabrowski was

shocked to see the ghostly likeness of General Lee sitting astride the lone horse. The apparition—clad in Lee's famed colonel's jacket and West Point cap—appeared at the end of the line of troops, gazing toward the battle.

"Shivers ran down my spine," Dabrowski said. "You can see right through the body. The woods and trees on the other side can be seen through the torso and hat and face area."

He added, "I wasn't sure what I had, but I knew it was something special."

Others who saw the photo agreed, including Dr. Mark Newell, a South Carolina archaeologist and photo expert, and Doug Smith, a computer expert. Both men inspected the original negative and verified their authenticity.

The photo was scanned into three separate computers by three different individuals who came up with identical results.

"It's the real thing," Smith said. "Chris captured something that day that is unexplainable."

While the ghosts of Jeb Stuart, Stonewall Jackson and other famous commanders have reportedly made appearances at Gettysburg, Shiloh, Cold Harbor and other battlefields, this is apparently the first time anyone has seen the specter of Robert E. Lee.

"Apparitions are pretty common on Civil War battlefields," noted Dabrowski. "To my knowledge, however, this is the first time Lee's ghost has been seen."

The ghostly figure "perfectly matches" better-known photos of General Lee that have appeared in books by historian Emory Thomas and others, Dabrowski added.

The controversial photo has been the subject of several newspaper articles and a recent NBC news program.

Dabrowski, a former newspaper reporter and graduate of Seton Hall University, says he will keep telling the story until he gets some answers.

"I won't rest until I get to the bottom of this mystery," he said.

A deeply religious man, Dabrowski said he and his family share a history of paranormal encounters. Cold drafts, phantom footsteps and poltergeist activity are all part of their experience.

"I believe in the possibility of ghosts," he said. "I am a journalist, a believer in truth and the rational explanation for most things. But there are some things that defy our imagination, and some people seem to be more receptive to spirits."

But the photo of General Lee's ghost has left him bewildered.

"Maybe his ghost still roams battlefields because he died an unhappy man," Dabrowski theorized. "Researchers at Northwestern University believe that unhappy spirits continue to roam the earth. Maybe Lee's spirit is not happy with the way turned out and is still beckoning the war cry."

◈

GHOST HOUSE

Gloomy Washington mansion infested
with angry spirits

The old house stood at the corner of 11th and D Streets
in a bleak and rundown section of Washington, D.C.
Before it was torn down by a frightened mob in the early
1900s, the ramshackle structure with the peeling paint
and broken windows was center stage for one of the most
famous paranormal events in American history.

For months people had complained about the foul
smells and strange sounds emanating from the deserted
house. Each time officers went to investigate they found
nothing out of the ordinary—except for the bones of
dead rats and cats and the fact that nothing green would
grow in the vacant lot surrounding the old house.

Some citizens thought the place was evil. How else to
explain the eerie howls of laughter, the maniacal shriek-
ing sounds they occasionally heard coming from the
house late at night?

Locals dubbed it the "Ghost House" because they felt
sure it was haunted by "angry spirits." Most people
stayed away from the place and warned their kids to stay
out of the gloomy yard overgrown with weeds and mis-
shapen trees.

Whenever a pet or child would go missing, people
blamed it on the Ghost House—even though no bodies
were ever found within its crumbling corridors.

No one really knew who owned the once grand structure, which dated back to the late 1860s. One story held that it had been built by a German immigrant who made a fortune in the furniture business during the Gilded Age.

For a while, the two-story building was the scene of lavish parties and cheerful laughter. Well-dressed visitors came and went, and rumors ran wild about the loud and raucous orgies said to be held behind its stately walls.

Sometimes around 1900 the house was abandoned. Its reputation as a haunted house apparently got started by prostitutes and vagabonds who sought refuge there. One woman claimed she saw a "black ghost" and another said she was attacked by a "big black dog" in the hallway.

The stories grew—and so did people's fear of the place.

When a couple of teenagers saw a "strange blue light" flickering in an upstairs window, the neighbors decided they'd had enough. They called in a priest to exorcise the place of demons.

Father Boyle of St. Patrick's Church was young and inexperienced, the unlikeliest of candidates for the job. But when the Church tapped him for the assignment, the young priest had no choice but to pack his exorcism gear and go to work.

Things started to go wrong the second he and his assistant opened the front door. First, an iron bar from the door flew into the air and crashed into a nearby wall. Other objects moved around the room "on their own accord, as if manipulated by unseen hands," according to Father Boyle.

Of particular concern was a chair that rose from the floor and floated toward them. The chair bumped the ceiling before settling back down to the floor. Father Boyle said a fire "roared up" in a fireplace, only to be extinguished a few seconds later.

The jittery pair went from room to room, tossing Holy War into the air and commanding the demons to vacate the premises. Every step of the way they were assaulted by moaning noises and "unclean odors."

At one point a door was ripped off its hinges and dropped to the floor. A rusting chandelier fell from the ceiling, narrowly missing the assistant.

But the ordeal was far from over. When Father Boyle started up the stairs leading to the attic, he encountered a "maniacal whirlwind" that "blew furniture around the room like cardboard."

The force of the wind drove Father Boyle back downstairs. There he found his assistant cowering in a corner—frightened out of his wits by the swirling mass of poltergeist activity.

Unwilling to risk further harm to himself or his comrade, Father Boyle fled the house. As he pulled the door shut behind him, he heard what sounded like "many harsh voices" laughing and jeering his exit.

A few days later, a group of men armed with Bibles and axes tore the Ghost House down. As far as anyone knows, the "angry spirits" of the Ghost House were never seen or heard from again.

GLAMIS CASTLE

Scottish castle cursed with monstrous entities

V ampires, witches, monsters and a fearsome menagerie of ghosts supposedly stalk the lonely corridors of Glamis Castle, the oldest inhabited castle in Scotland and childhood home of Queen Elizabeth II.

Paranormal investigators say the sprawling, multi-towered castle situated near the village of Glamis five miles west of Forfar is the most haunted building in the world. Strange occurrences date back to the Eighth Century when Glamis was a holy place occupied by a legendary saint named Fergus.

The actual structure, built in the Fourteenth Century as a hunting lodge for Scottish kings, was also the legendary setting for Shakespeare's Macbeth. Regarded as the most beautiful castle in the world, the estate had fallen into ruins by the mid-Seventeenth Century due to unwise investments and the notorious gambling habits of its owners, the "lords of Glamis."

In 1677 Patrick Lyons inherited the place—along with his ancestors' massive debts. It took forty years of hard work to turn the family fortune around, for which he was awarded the title, Earl of Strathmore.

In the early 1800s, according to legend, the Strathmores were confronted with an unpleasant situation. The first son of the 11th Earl of Strathmore was born a hideously deformed, egg-shaped monster with no neck, tiny arms and legs, and a large, hairy torso.

The "Monster of Glamis," as he became known, was the true heir to the family estate. Ashamed of the creature, however, the family locked him away in a secret chamber. His actual existence was a closely guarded secret, known only by the family lawyer and succeeding generations of Earl of Strathmore who were shown the creature on their 21st birthday.

It is said that the monster lived a remarkably long life and died in the 1930s.

In 1880, newspapers reported that a workman accidentally broke through a wall and found the monster's locked room. The workman supposedly disappeared a short time later, along with a large sum of money and a ticket to Australia.

The most famous ghostly occupant of the castle is said to be Alexander Lindsay, the fourth earl of Strathmore—better known as Earl Beardie—who supposedly sold his soul to the Devil during a card game. Sounds of stamping, swearing and the rattling of dice are occasionally heard drifting from the tower where Earl Beardie cursed God and challenged the Devil to a game of cards.

Other ghosts include that of Janet Douglas, wife of the sixth lord of Glamis, who poisoned her husband, James, in 1531. Six years later she was burned at the stake as a witch after trying to poison King James V.

Janet's ghost appears above the clock tower, wrapped in flames or a reddish glow. On stormy nights, another ghost—that of a mad-man—can be seen walking along the roof near a spot called "The Mad Earl's Walk."

Many visitors have reported encounters with unidentified "gray ladies" who supposedly haunt the chapel. A "tongue-less woman" has also been seen racing across the grounds at midnight, tearing at her mouth.

The spirit of a young African boy—thought to have been a badly treated page—often sits on a stone seat in the hallway outside the Queen Mother's sitting room. A woman with "mournful eyes" has been spotted peering down from an open window and a tall figure dressed in a long, dark cloak is occasionally seen in the courtyard.

Glamis's vampire is said to be a woman servant who was caught sucking the blood of a victim. Legend has it that she was walled up alive in a secret chamber, where she continues to sleep the sleep of the undead, until someone finds her and she is loosed once again.

Two famous murders are said to have been perpetrated at Glamis Castle—Macbeth's slaying of King Duncan, mentioned in Shakespeare's *Macbeth*, and that of King Malcolm II, who reigned during the Eleventh Century, three centuries before the castle was built. Lore has it that a mysterious bloodstain from Malcolm's murder could not be scrubbed off the floor, and the entire floor in the room had to be boarded over.

Modern poltergeist phenomena include eerie screams, banging noises, bedclothes mysteriously ripped off beds at night and doors that refuse to stay closed, even after being bolted and hammered shut.

GRANNY'S GHOST

Elderly woman's spirit won't leave home

Shortly after she and her family moved into the spooky old house near Eastman, Georgia, Betty Kight saw a "thin, stoop-shouldered old woman" standing in a flower bed outside her kitchen window.

"She was just standing there in the canna lilies looking right at me," Kight said.
"When I went outside, she was gone."

Neighbors told her not to worry—it was only the ghost of Mrs. Sammy King, an elderly woman who died in the house more than eighty years ago after being struck by lightning.

They described Mrs. King as a kindly grandmother who loved children and flowers, especially the canna lilies that grew outside the kitchen. In the late 1920s, she was sitting near a window in the kitchen shelling peas when a bolt of lightning struck, killing her instantly.

According to some, her spirit still haunts the property.

Betty Kight saw the specter six more times—each lasting longer than the one before. Always clad in dark colors and wearing an old-fashioned bonnet, the ghostly figure was seen picking flowers, gathering twigs and cones, and even sitting on the porch of her old house.

"She always wears a long brown dress with long sleeves and a scarf or bonnet that hides her face," Betty said. "And she's usually surrounded by a soft haze of smoke."

Her favorite spot was the flower bed.

"The first time I saw her, I was in the kitchen putting things away when I looked through the window and saw this little old lady standing in the canna lilies," she said . "When I went outside, she was gone."

After the sixth sighting, Betty said she got so afraid she chopped down the canna lilies. That didn't stop the haunting, however.

"It got worse," Betty explained. "The ghost started visiting my children, even in broad daylight."

Although husband Bob has never actually seen the ghost, Betty says her children—all of whom grew up in the house—have.

"One day my son Robert heard singing, so he went out on the porch. There sat Mrs. King in the swing with three children around her singing out of a song book," Betty noted.

There have been many other encounters with the ghostly apparition, including one by daughter Elaine that still leaves Betty's hair on end.

"One night after supper Elaine started out to feed the dogs. She opened the door with a plate of scraps in her hands, and there stood Mrs. King. Elaine screamed and threw the plate in the floor and slammed the door," Betty said.

Apparently, members of the Kight family were only the latest in a long list of people who say they have seen Mrs. King's ghost. Other witnesses say they've seen a "little old woman wearing a scarf or bonnet" floating or gliding across the property.

Betty said she never believed in ghosts until the arrival of Mrs. King's spirit.

"I thought it was a lot of nonsense," she said.

At first, the Kights had no idea who—or what—the ghost was that haunted their property. Later, after talking with neighbors and relatives of the old house's former owners, they learned that their spectral visitor was probably Mrs. Sammy King, a kind, gracious woman who had been struck by lightning and killed sometime in the late 1920s.

Descriptions of Mrs. King, said Betty, matched that of her ghost from the top of her bonnet to the heels of her black, lace-up shoes.

But a decade of the haunting was enough for her and her family. In 1973, they built a new house about 100 yards from the old house and moved in, hoping they might be rid of their unwanted visitor from beyond. Two weeks after settling in, however, more strange things started happening.

Flickering lights were spotted in the window of the old woman's room across the way. Moaning, sobbing sounds were sometimes heard outside in the yard at night.

Then the ghost began to make its presence known in the new house. At first it was only the opening and closing of doors and moving things around that bothered the Kights. Soon there were more sightings—so many, in fact, the Kights thought of bringing in an exorcist.

They never did.

Instead, the Kights began to grow fond of the kindly old presence that continues to fade in and out of view at unpredicted moments.

"We've just accepted the fact that she's here," Betty explained.

Now, instead of running or being afraid, the Kights

consider the ghost part of the family.

"She's friendly, and she doesn't want to hurt us," Betty added. "I almost feel like she's part of the family."

In the beginning, the harassed family thought of selling their haunted home and moving away—far away, so the ghost wouldn't follow. After a while, they changed their minds.

"I really think she's attached to us," Betty noted, adding that she believes the ghost of Mrs. King still haunts the property because "she didn't finish her mission here on earth."

GRAY MAN

Solemn specter patrol's Carolina beaches

F ew sights are more chilling to residents along the Carolina coast than an appearance by the so-called Gray Man, a silent, solemn specter said to materialize shortly before the arrival of a hurricane.

Hundreds of beach-goers and homeowners along the Grand Strand sat they've seen the ghost. He's usually described as a somber little man dressed in an old-fashioned hat and long, gray coat. Many witnesses swear the sightings came within days or even hours of a major storm.

"He's real, " said Matt Rodgers, a Boston insurance executive who vacations at Pawleys Island, a historical community about thirty-five miles northeast of Georgetown. "I've seen him several times with my own eyes. So have other members of my family."

Rodgers said he first saw the Gray Man in 1971, the first year he rented a beachfront house.

"It was early one morning," Rodgers said. "I was alone on the beach, watching the waves and birds. Suddenly, I looked behind me, and there he was. He was a little man, about five feet tall, standing about thirty yards up the beach. He was dressed in a quaint, old-fashioned suit, complete with long tails, hat and tie. Then he vanished, right before my eyes."

The startled Bostonian never told anyone about the apparition. In fact, he forgot about it until the late 1980's, right before Hurricane Hugo struck.

"My brother was down from Charlotte, and we were out walking the beach, looking for shark's teeth," Rodgers explained. "We happened to turn around and saw him at the same time, the same little gray man I had seen some fifteen years earlier. Then he vanished again, just like he did before."

It wasn't until after Hugo slammed into the Carolina coast a few weeks later that Rodgers heard about the "curse of the Gray Man." According to legend, the property and lives of people who see the Gray Man are mysteriously spared from storms.

Just how the legend got started is unclear, but some researchers think it originated in the early 1800s when a young man sailing down from New England to meet his bride near Charleston drowned after his ship sank in a storm. The Gray Man is said to be the young man's ghost patrolling the shore to warn others about impending bad weather.

Variations of the story say it is a "Gray Woman" instead of a "Gray Man" who haunts the lonely beaches. Said to be the bride-to-be of the doomed young man, her spirit roams the beaches in search of her dead lover. Like the Gray Man, she sometimes appears to warn mortals that a storm is rolling in.

Other coastal regions have their own versions of the Gray Man story, but none has received the notoriety of South Carolina's famed specter. Sightings have been made from Myrtle Beach south to Edisto Island and Hilton Head. The apparition is frequently spotted strolling the dunes at Fripp Island.

The most memorable warnings came shortly before powerful storms hit the South Carolina coast in

September 1822, October 1893 and October 1954. In each case, several people reported seeing a strange little man dressed in gray clothes walking the stormy beach just hours before the storms truck.

In 1954 an automobile dealer named Bill Collins had an encounter with the Gray Man near his beachfront home at Pawleys Island.

"I was looking down from my deck when I saw a strangely dressed little man looking right up at me," Collins said. "I knew in my heart I was having a genuine out-of-this-world experience.

A few days later Hurricane Hazel blew in from the south, washing away scores of beachfront houses. But Collin's house was spared—indisputable proof that the man in the gray had come to warn him.

HAUNTED INDIAN MOUND

Strange bumps in the night

Thirteen years ago, Lynne and Mark Wisner bought twenty acres of land near Grovetown, Georgia, and built their dream home, a two-story, contemporary A-frame in a woodsy setting that included several creeks, stands of hardwoods and a gently sloping meadow.

They loved their new house—and the peace and quiet.

"It was almost like heaven," Lynne recounted in an interview.

One of the things that appealed to them about the property was an old Indian mound located about fifty yards behind the house at the edge of a swamp bordering Euchee Creek. The mound, which rises to about twenty feet in the middle, has never been properly excavated, although numerous Indian relics have been found in the area.

The Wisners think it's a burial mound.

They also think it is haunted.

Strange lights, eerie drumbeats, chanting and phantom figures dancing in the woods after sundown are among the ghostly goings-on that have plagued the Wisners over the years.

"It started soon after we moved in," Lynne recalled. "We'd hear these noises, like drums out in the woods, and they sometimes lasted for hours."

She said the drumbeats were usually followed by what sounded like chanting sounds.

"We'd go out in the back yard to investigate, but we'd never find anything to explain what was going on," she said. "The drumbeats were real scary. It was like somebody beating on a hollow log."

On several occasions the Wisners saw "ghost lights" flickering near the barn in the back yard. Lynne noted that it always happened at night, usually after the family had gone to bed.

"Imagine getting up in the middle of the night, looking out in the back yard and seeing this strange light going up and down just outside your window," she said.

The eerie incidents have left some family members so shaken they refuse to go out at night.

"It's scary," admitted Lynne, an artist and stay-at-home mom who raises horses and cats. "Anytime you experience strange things like this and can't find a logical reason for it, it bothers you a lot."

A few years ago she looked out her window and saw "ghost-like figures" dancing around the mound. The figures appeared to "float above the ground, like smoke," Lynne said, and were accompanied by chanting and drumbeats.

"It was not my imagination," she said emphatically. "It nearly scared me to death. All of us have seen similar things—my husband, daughter and son-in-law. My son-in-law, in fact, will not stay in this house alone anymore."

None of the farm animals will go near the mound. One of the horses, Dancer, often refuses to let anyone get close to the gloomy pile of earth.

"He'll throw a fit and block my way," she said. "One

time he was relentless, throwing his head around, rearing up, snorting and stamping his feet. He would not let me go near that mound."

Some friends have urged the Wisners to destroy—or, at least, excavate—the old mound. But the Wisners say they have no plans for either.

"That old mound has been here a lot longer than we have," they explained. "We have no desire, no reason now to take it apart."

HAUNTED JAIL

Young killer's spirit hangs around Texas cell

In 1979, a convicted killer serving time at the Bailey County Jailhouse in Muleshoe, Texas, tied a strip of towels together and hanged himself from an air grate in the ceiling. Lawmen said the youthful felon committed suicide because he didn't want to go to the gas chamber or spend the rest of his life behind bars.

"That was the end of him," said Benny Clifton, a former sheriff's deputy. "Or, so we thought."

Now some officers and inmates aren't so sure. Many think the ghost of the young murderer has come back to haunt the jail.

It all started a few days after the hanging when other inmates reported hearing strange noises. Some saw shadows where none should have been. One frightened inmate swore he saw a disembodied "bloody hand" hovering over his bunk one night.

At first, jailers laughed the stories off. They thought the convicts were just making them up to get attention or to pull fast ones on the guards. Things changed, however, when officers starting experiencing weird phenomena themselves—banging and scraping sounds in deserted cells, flashing lights, odd footsteps, cold spots and other strange manifestations.

Most of the bizarre activity occurred late at night, but daytime reports of eerie happenings were not uncommon. One relative of an inmate was frightened out of his wits during a noonday visit when he felt a "strange, prickly feeling" at the base of his neck.

Parapsychologists were brought in. Using high-tech sensors, tape recorders, video cameras and other electronic equipment, the investigators detected strange drops in temperature throughout the old jailhouse. Their conclusion: The building was probably occupied by a "disturbing presence," perhaps a "lost and confused spirit."

The haunting has brought fame to Muleshoe, population 5,000. Requests for information about the ghost have come from as far away as Canada and China.

"It's world-famous," noted Clifton. "People come here from all over to learn more about this thing—newspaper reporters and TV types, mostly. But we get a lot of ordinary curiosity seekers too."

The twenty-year veteran of law enforcement added, "We're the only county jail in Texas that plays host to a ghost."

Thomas Yanis might have been the first person to hear the ghost. It happened late one night while the 22-year-old inmate was curled up on his bunk reading.

"I heard something in the next cell shuffling around," Yanis recounted to *Fate Magazine.* "I heard it move around on a bed I knew was empty. And that right there put me on my knees praying."

On another occasion, several other inmates said they saw the ghost pass by their cell late one night.

"It was dark, like a person's shadow," said Manuel Venegas. "The shadow moved to the back of the central holding cell and down a hallway with only one exit. We waited for whoever it was to come up from the hallway, but nobody did."

Venegas didn't sleep well that night.

"That thing gave me goosebumps," he explained. "I don't argue with anybody now. I don't cause no trouble because I don't want to come back to this jail."

Former Sheriff Jerry Hicks doesn't believe in ghosts, but he said he was glad the dead man's spirit helped keep the prisoners quiet.

"I'd have to see something tangible to be convinced we had a ghost here," he said. "But I can say that things are quieter back there in the cells since this has started. There's more Bible reading going on than ever before."

Cecil Campbell, a psychologist with the Texas Department of Corrections, said it's not uncommon for felons to be more superstitious than the general population.

"So, in a way, ghosts have the power to keep inmates in line without even being seen," Dr. Campbell said. "Personally, I think it's a hoot."

One mass sighting of the ghost occurred when a group of inmates seated at a dining table said they heard—then saw—a dark form gliding in the corner of the room.

"Everybody stopped eating and talking," one inmate noted. "When we looked over and saw nothing real there, we knew it was the ghost."

HAUNTED NEWSPAPER

Staffers spooked by dapper snoop

When most people think about ghosts, they think about drafty old houses, crumbling castles and mist-shrouded graveyards.

Rarely do newspaper offices come to mind. It's hard to associate the clean clatter of Linotype machines and the electronic hum of modern video terminals with rattling chains, moaning noises and phantom footsteps echoing down unlit hallways.

But don't try to tell that to the people who work for the *Sullivan County News*. Some reporters, editors and other staffers of the Blountville, Tennessee, weekly claim the place is haunted.

For the past five decades, *News* workers have told harrowing stories about doors opening and shutting mysteriously, footsteps clomping around on the second floor, eerie whistling sounds echoing through the basement and spectral shadows flitting across the cluttered newsroom. Before the arrival of computer terminals, Linotype machines would sometimes suddenly start up by themselves.

It got so spooky that one former editor grabbed his pistol and fired twice at something he thought was a ghost.

"And we're all the time missing things," complained

June Eaton, the advertising supervisor. "They'll be there, and all of a sudden, you won't see them—scissors, flowers, pencils, anything."

Thelma Harrington, a former editor, said she was working in the darkroom alone one night when she heard a strange, whistling sound. Thinking it was a friend, she went outside to investigate.

"I opened the door and called his name," she said. "He didn't respond. I looked out in the parking lot and his car wasn't there. So I went back into the darkroom, and the whistling started again."

After searching the entire building, she simply concluded: "Nobody was there."

Other witnesses include Glen and Melvin Boyd, brothers who worked as printers until they retired several years ago. Both tell of constantly hearing footsteps clomping around at night on the upper floor while they were working down in the print shop.

Each time they went up to investigate, they'd find the door locked and no one there. Encounters such as these are routinely shared by other staffers. In fact, the mysterious sounds on the first floor became so common—especially late at night—that most workers stopped going up to investigate.

"I must have gone up a hundred times," Melvin said, "and there was nobody there. Usually we didn't bother to go upstairs. In fact, if somebody actually had come in, the people downstairs would be very startled."

One of the most bizarre encounters involved a young editor who had just started work at the paper. According to Glen Boyd, the editor was working late one night when he heard the Linotype machine start up by itself.

The young editor "thought it was me," said Boyd,

"and he came down to talk to me. But I was out covering a story. When he got downstairs, nobody was there. But now he could hear something upstairs, someone walking around. He went upstairs, but there was no one there and he went back to his office."

At that moment the front door suddenly sprang open by itself.

"It got to a point where it shook him up," Boyd went on. "He had a pistol in his desk drawer, and he got it out and went out into the main room. He didn't see anybody, but the newspaper files were moving, as though somebody was flipping through them. He had a little .25 automatic gun, and he had his finger on the trigger, and it went off twice, putting two bullet holes in the ceiling. The marks are still there."

Some people say they have actually seen the ghost—known around the office as "George." A former printer named Jim Gose once described a tall, slender man dressed in a gray suit who came into the office through the back door, walked ten steps toward the stairs, went upstairs and then vanished.

Thelma Harrington, the former editor, has seen her share of apparitions at the newspaper.

"One time," she said, "I saw a person in the office across the hall from my office. It appeared to be a young man with blond hair and a crew cut, which was not usual for that time—crew cuts were long past. He was wearing a white oxford shirt and blue pants with pleats in front. All of that stuff was completely out of style at that time."

When she went to ask if she could help him, the young man disappeared. A quick check through the rest of the building turned up nothing.

"The whole place was empty," she said.

Predictably, theories abound as to the origin and nature of the ghost. The most popular notion is that the phantom is that of a young man said to have been killed back in the 1940s when the newspaper building was a pool hall.

"There were a lot of stabbings and shootings back then," one reporter noted. "If someone was killed—and that's a very real possibility—that person's spirit still might be hanging around, haunting the place."

The best time to see the ghost, say *News* staffers who believe, is late at night and on weekends when few people are around. Arthur Myers, author of *The Ghostly Gazetteer*, has looked into the haunting and reports that manifestations can be experienced any time of day or night.

"The opening and closing of front doors seems to happen often during usual working houses," he said. "The footsteps are more discernible during the evening or on weekends, when only one or two people are in the building."

It's been years since the haunted newspaper made news, and that's just fine with staffers less than eager for the ghost to return.

HAW BRANCH PLANTATION

The portrait that dripped blood

Ghostly visitations, blood-curling screams in the night, sinister birds and macabre portraits that dripped blood are just some of the spooky goings-on said to have plagued Haw Branch Plantation, a handsome old manor house near Amelia, Virginia, since Civil War times.

Unexplained disturbances continue, but the plantation owners have long since lost their fear.

"It's something we've learned to live with," commented Gibson McConnaughey, who bought the estate in 1964, "but at times it does get frightening."

In antebellum days, Haw Branch Plantation was a 15,000-acre estate, complete with slave quarters and a dry moat. After the war, the plantation fell into disuse and ruin.

In 1964, Mrs. McConnaughey bought the property, which had once belonged to her grandmother. Mrs. McConnaughey remembers playing in the house as a child, but for the past fifty years or so, no one in the family had lived there.

Restoration was tedious. Not only did the main house, with its tall brick chimney and brooding columns, undergo massive rehabilitation, but acres of fields and rolling yards had to be cut back and preened. Finally, after four years of hard work, one of the South's most noted architectural gems was gleaming again.

Then the portrait arrived.

The subject was a beautiful young woman, said to be a distant, long-dead relative named Florence Wright. When the portrait was uncrated, the McConnaugheys were astonished to find a dingy black and white charcoal drawing rather than the brilliant pastel they were promised by a cousin who gave it to them as a housewarming gift.

Mrs. McConnaughey dutifully hung the portrait over the library mantel anyway, thinking how much her ancestor would have appreciated it. Less than a month later, she made a startling discovery—the portrait was starting to become colorized!

Even more amazing, at certain times, the portrait appeared to drip blood at the lower-right hand corner of the canvas.

Bewildered and frightened, she called in her husband and several visitors to witness the phenomenon. Incredibly, over the next few weeks, fresh and living color began to creep into almost every gray and black tone in the picture.

It was as if the "dead" portrait had been brought back to life inside the old house.

Accompanying the eerie changes on the canvas were strange, blood-curdling sounds, mostly of a woman screaming from upstairs in the attic. The sounds continued, but the McConnaugheys soon became concerned about a new phenomenon.

In 1967, they began to notice the apparition of a young woman flitting down the hallway stairs. The McConnaugheys finally identified the spirit—always clad in a full-length white dress—as Harriet Mason, their great-grandmother.

On other occasions family members saw what looked like an old man carrying a kerosene lantern across the yard. They also heard the ghostly tinkling of cow-bells circling the house, even though there were no cows on the property.

One of the most frightening events occurred when the phantom of an enormous white bird with a wingspan of more than six feet appeared on their lawn. The last strange sighting has been that of a cavalier gentleman in riding boots who screamed, "Help me!"

None of the strange events have ever been sufficiently explained to the McConnaughey family, who continue to reside in one of America's most famous haunted houses.

◈

HEADLESS COWBOY

Phantom rider brought terror to Old West

Out of the west Texas badlands of the Rio Nueces and across the pages of Wild West lore galloped the dreaded "headless rider," a mysterious, mounted specter that brought fear and terror to a generation of ranchers and cowboys during the mid-Nineteenth Century.

Hundreds of people claimed to have seen the ghostly rider roaming the lonely ranges on a black mustang stallion with glowing red eyes. Clad in rawhide leggings and a buckskin jacket, the figure often appeared out of nowhere, sometimes accompanied by wind and thunder.

The sight of the headless specter was enough to frighten even the bravest gunslinger.

The most gruesome feature about the solitary rider was that he had no head, only a gaping hole atop his shoulders where his neck should have been. According to legend, the mysterious phantom carried his decapitated head on the front of his saddle, lashed to the horn beneath a sombrero.

So many stories cropped up about the nocturnal rider it seems likely that more than one headless cowboy stalked the plains. Most of the sightings occurred in the area around the Rio Nueces in the southwestern part of the state, a dismal, canyon-pocked region inhabited by rattlesnakes, scorpions and wild mustangs.

Some frontiersmen swore the rider was alive—an outlaw, perhaps, who donned grisly attire for the purpose of terrorizing the population. Others said it was the ghost of a *vaquero*—a Mexican cowboy—whose spiritual mission was to guard the lost gold mine of the abandoned Candelaria Mission on the Rio Nueces.

A less fanciful theory proposed that the ghost was a mounted scarecrow whose job was to stampede mares into exhaustion, after which they could be easily rounded up by cowboys.

The real answer came one day when a group of ranchers gathered to lie in wait for the rider at one of its favorite haunts. That afternoon, as the apprehensive gunmen crouched behind rocks and sagebrush, a powerful thunderstorm swept in. Lightning flashed and thunder rumbled through the canyon while the ambushers waited.

Without warning, the dreaded horseman appeared, galloping at a heart-stopping pace toward the terrified men lying in wait. Not knowing what to do, the bushwhackers cut loose with rifles and six-guns.

When the smoke and dust had cleared, horse and rider lay sprawled in a grotesque heap.

Advancing cautiously, they made a startling discovery—the black stallion was nothing more than a plain horse, now shot dead, and the rider was actually the dried-up corpse of some cowboy strapped in the saddle.

The corpse was riddled with hundreds of bullets and other wounds from arrows and spears. Beneath the rotting sombrero was a small skull, shriveled away from many years in the grueling Western sun.

Ranchers later leaned that the dead man was Vidal, a convicted horse thief who had operated throughout much of the Southwest until his untimely end.

Vidal's free-wheeling crime spree had apparently

ended when a rancher named Creed Taylor killed him for trying to steal some of his horses. To set an example for other would-be rustlers, the dead cowboy was strapped to the horse and sent galloping off across the desert.

As a final fitting touch, Taylor ordered one of his men, Bigfoot Wallace, to chop off Vidal's head and strap the outlaw's body to a wild stallion. The head was affixed to the saddle horn beneath a large sombrero.

The headless rider story is sometimes confused with another famous legend about phantom cowboys who haunted the Texas plains in the 1870s. It was these "Ghost Riders" who inspired the popular song, *Ghost Riders in the Sky*.

WASHINGTON IRVING

Literary great returns to finish book

D<small>r.</small> J.G. Cogswell often worked alone in New York's Astor Library, sometimes late at night when most of the staff and visitors had gone home.

One night in 1859, long after the library had shut down, the elderly physician was pouring over some documents in a remote corner of the building when he was startled by a noise a few aisles over.

Since no one else was supposed to be in the library, he strolled over to investigate. When he rounded the corner of a bookshelf, he was surprised to see an old man hunched over a table reading a book in the main gallery.

There wasn't much light in the room—just enough for Dr. Cogswell to recognize someone vaguely familiar about the frail stranger half-hidden in the shadows. As he approached to inquire how the elderly gentleman had entered the locked building, the doctor couldn't shake the feeling that he somehow knew the man.

Then it hit him—the quaintly clad reader was his old friend, Washington Irving, the famous author who had helped found the library and often used its facilities.

But that was impossible. Washington Irving, the man who had given the world *The Legend of Sleepy Hollow*, *Rip Van Winkle* and a dozen other literary masterpieces, was dead—had been dead for several months. Dr.

Cogswell had even gone to his funeral!

Understandably, the doctor almost collapsed. It took him a few seconds to recover, but by that time the ghostly form of his friend had disappeared.

Shaken, Dr. Cogswell decided it was in his best interest not to tell anyone what he had seen. Who would believe him?

A few nights later, he was again working late in the library. The last group of visitors had left hours earlier, and he was alone among the shifting shadows and creaking sounds of the musty old building.

His reverie was suddenly interrupted by a strange noise—the same kind of noise he had heard the night the ghost of Washington Irving appeared. He looked up and, sure enough, there stood his old friend again, white-haired head bent gracefully over a book.

The ghost, half-hidden in the shadows, seemed oblivious to the doctor's presence. Determined to speak to it this time, Cogswell tiptoed over, so as not to frighten or startle the apparition.

Before he drew any closer, however, the ethereal presence started to fade—slowly at first, then faster and faster until there was nothing left but a few transparent patches of misty gray hovering over the book. They, too, finally disappeared, and the book crashed mysteriously to the floor.

When Cogswell later told some friends what he had seen in the library, they kindly encouraged him to go to the country for a few days of rest.

A couple of weeks later, a library user reported seeing a similar apparition. Then, in early 1860, Irving's own nephew, Pierre Irving, told friends that he had also seen his late uncle's ghost, only this time it was at the Irving home in Tarrytown, New York, instead of the library.

In the years that followed, numerous other sightings of Irving's ghost were reported, mostly at the Astor Library. Through the early 1860s, while the nation was engaged in a bloody Civil War, New York newspapers frequently carried stories about the apparition alongside front page reports from the battlefield.

The European press also picked up the eerie story. As the first American author to gain international recognition, Irving had become a favorite among literary circles in England, France and Germany.

That's why so many fans, including Europeans, were fascinated by his own ghost story. This was the man, it should be recalled, who had written *The Legend of Sleepy Hollow*, a hair-raising tale about haunted woods, demons and a headless horseman.

Drawing-room wisdom had it that Irving had returned from the dead to complete an unfinished novel he had been working on just before he died. There were also those who maintained that the ghost was only having fun, and that it was just like the prank-loving author to cause so much commotion from the other side of the grave.

Irving would probably have gotten a big kick out of all the gossipy ghost stories circulated among New York's high society. It is ironic that the impish author, who didn't believe in the supernatural himself, was not only the author of America's first ghost story—*Sleepy Hollow*—but would also become the subject of New York's most celebrated ghost tale.

LADY LOVIBOND

Ghost schooner still sails the English coast

"It came straight out of the fog like a moldy shadow, its rotted old timbers creaking and groaning, its ripped and mangled sails flapping and cracking in the cold night wind like the laughter of Satan himself..."

That's how English sea captain Bull Prestwick described his encounter with one of England's most famous ghost ships, the *Lady Lovibond*, a three-masted schooner that went down with all hands on February 13, 1748, about five miles off the Kent coast near the village of Deal.

Prestwick and several of his crewmen reportedly watched the phantom ship glide toward them for about five minutes before it vanished in the fog.

"She looked real enough," Prestwick said about the ship, "but there was a curious green glow about her that gave us all a bad fright."

Prestwick's 1948 account is similar to dozens of others reported over the years. According to legend, the *Lady Lovibond* reappears every fifty years on February 13 and is usually seen running aground near the same spot where it sank more than 250 years ago.

On its first appearance in 1798, the crew on at least two ships reported seeing it. The phantom was so real that the master of the coaster *Edenbridge* thought his ship nearly collided with it.

In 1848, the phantom made another appearance.

Again, it was so real that Deal seamen thought a wreck had actually occurred and set out in lifeboats to rescue survivors. None were found, nor were any traces of a wrecked ship.

According to Christina Hole, author of *Haunted England*, the ship was cursed from the beginning because a woman was on board.

"In the superstitions of sailing, it has always been considered bad luck to take a woman to sea," Hole said. "In the case of the *Lady Lovibond*, the captain's young bride, Annetta, was on board."

One version of the story holds that the first mate secretly loved Annetta and deliberately wrecked the ship for revenge.

"Many Deal old-timers familiar with the tale say this first mate killed the helmsman, then ran the ship onto the sands where they all perished because he couldn't have Annetta," said Rosemary Ellen Guiley, author of *The Encyclopedia of Ghosts and Spirits*. "On cold winter nights sailors still gather at taverns to debate who was to blame."

Numerous other phantom ship sightings have been reported in the same area, including that of the *SS Violet*, a paddle steamer that ran aground crossing the English channel in a snowstorm more than a century years ago. Everyone on board was killed, including two pregnant sisters who supposedly lashed themselves to the deck to keep from being swept overboard.

During World War II, sailors from several ships reportedly saw the ill-fated ship and heard the screams of the two women. The sightings were so vivid that lifeboats were sent out to investigate.

The frequency of ghost ship sightings off the Kent

coast has made that region one of the most haunted in the world. According to lore, this dangerous spot was once the island of Lomea, which was flooded and drowned in the Eleventh Century when the Earl of Goodwin neglected to maintain its sea walls.

There is no evidence that such an island ever existed, yet on certain nights the phantom bells of its drowned churches reportedly can be heard tolling beneath the sea. Legend also has it that some 50,000 people have lost their lives in shipwrecks on the sandbank.

LEMP MANSION

Fame and fortune couldn' t protect prominent St. Louis family from curse

The Lemp family of St. Louis seemed to have it all--money, fame and power beyond the average person's wildest dream. As owners of one of the nation's leading beer breweries, the Lemp clan reigned supreme at the top of St. Louis society, wielding uncommon political and financial clout during the so-called Gilded Age.

All that began to change in 1901 when 28-year-old Frederick Lemp, heir apparent to the family fortune, dropped dead of a heart attack. Some said he had worked himself to death. Others believed he was the victim of a curse—a curse that brought death and depression to the Lemp dynasty and ultimately destroyed their once-powerful empire.

William Lemp Sr. was devastated by the loss of his favorite son. For years, he had been grooming Frederick to take over the family business. Although he had five other children, "Freddy" was the one he had chosen to lead Lemp Brewery into the Twentieth Century.

William had inherited the company from his own father, a German immigrant named Adam Lemp who founded the brewery in 1838. Hard work and wise management helped transform the fledgling enterprise into one of the most prosperous breweries in the United States. By the time of the Civil War, the Lemp name was synonymous with quality beer. Americans loved the full-bodied, German-style lager and bought lots of it, making the Lemps one of the nation's richest families.

After his own father's death in 1862, William Lemp bought a fashionable Italiante mansion in the heart of St. Louis. The sprawling, 33-room showplace served as an auxiliary office as well as primary residence. They stuffed the house with art treasures from around the world and threw lavish parties for friends and fellow captains of industry.

The Lemp Mansion was as impressive underground as it was above. A tunnel, called Cherokee Cave, connected the main house with the brewery and featured a ballroom, heated swimming pool and theater auditorium. A zoo was added for the entertainment pleasure of guests.

Ironically, young Frederick's death came at the height of the family's greatest success. Unable to cope with the loss of his son, William--wildly eccentric even in the best of times--stopped going to work and gradually retreated from society altogether. In 1904, three years after Frederick's suicide, William slumped into his Lemp Mansion office and shot himself to death.

A dark cloud now seemed to settle over the Lemp Mansion. In 1920, daughter Elsa, depressed over business concerns and a failed marriage, placed a revolver against her chest and pulled the trigger. William Lemp Jr., next in line to inherit the business, took over the mansion and brewery. He expanded the house and stuffed it with so many treasures he built three large vaults for storage when they were away.

In 1899, Will married Lillian Handlan, the daughter of a prominent St. Louis manufactuer, who seemed to enjoy helping her socialite husband spend Lemp money. William eventually grew tired of his trophy wife, nicknamed the "Lavendar Lady" because of her fondness for the color, and divorced her. Their lavish lifestyle had always been the subject of St. Louis gossip; their dramatic parting was the talk of the town for years. When it was over, the "Lavendar Lady" went into seclusion, never to be seen in public again.

Will remarried, but his life was never the same again. He became melancholy and more reclusive. Like his father, he avoided contact with people, using the tunnel beneath the house to walk back and forth to worth.

Prohibition brought disaster to the brewery. Unable--or unwilling--to accept change and modernize, the Lemp Brewery shut down in 1922, losing millions in the process. Shortly after the company's assets were sold to an international shoe company, Will went into the same office that his father had nearly two decades before and shot himself in the chest with a revolver.

The fourth Lemp to commit suicide was Charles, Will's equally eccentric brother whose morbid fascination for the mansion and phobia against germs made him the strangest member of the family. In 1949, at the age of 77, he took his favorite dog down into the basement, shot it in the head, then turned the gun on himself.

Charles' death was the final blow to the once mighty Lemp empire. The mansion, which had long suffered from neglect, was sold and turned into a boarding house. In 1975, the property was purchased by a St. Louis businessman whose dream was to convert it into a bed and breakfast.

It was during the mansion's renovation that the weirdest part of the Lemp family saga was played out. Workers soon started complaining about banging noises and objects moving around on their own. Tools went missing for no apparent reason. Materials would vanish. Some felt "cold, clammy hands" on them in certain parts of the house. It was, said one, "as if unseen eyes were following you around, everywhere you went in that place."

Windows and doors opened and fell shut at random. Eerie laughter echoed through empty parts of the building. A lady dressed in lavendar was seen gliding down a stairway, then vanished in full view of several startled workers. Some said they heard the barking of a phantom dog, while others told of "piano noises" coming from upstairs.

Many workers quit, rather than face the eerie happenings. Word soon spread that the Lemp Mansion was haunted. Curiosity-seekers reportedly encountered "cold spots" in the house and heard disembodied voices and strange, rustling noises upstairs.

In 1980, LIFE Magazine called the Lemp Mansion "one of the most haunted houses in America."

Today, the fully restored Lemp Mansion is a popular inn and restaurant. It's checkered past has also helped make it a major tourist attraction. Customers and staffers often talk about dishes flying through the air and strange footsteps walking up and down the several flights of stairs.

Down in the cave, visitors have heard unearthly howling sounds. Some paranormal experts suggest it is the ghost of exotic animals once housed in the zoo. Others say it is only the ghost of "The Monkey Boy"—a mentally retarded, horribly deformed child spawned by William Jr. According to legend, the illegitimate child was kept locked in the cave all its life to avoid humiliation or disgrace.

The Lemp Mansion's dark past is only a memory

now. People still come looking for ghosts, but owner Paul Pointer says the house's main attraction is its wonderful food and comfortable lodging facilities.

"People come here expecting to experience weird things," he told Troy Taylor, author of *Ghost of the Prairie*, "and, fortunately for us, they are rarely disappointed."

LINDEN ROW INN

The sound of children laughing

Something strange stalks the long, dark corridors of the Linden Row Inn, a handsome, old hotel situated in the heart of Richmond, Virginia.

That "something" is said to mysteriously turn television sets on and off in guest rooms, slam doors, yank covers off beds, rattle doorknobs, moan and stomp around hallways in the dead of night. It also giggles and makes chuckling sounds in the dark.

Most chilling, perhaps, is the occasional laughter—said to be that of children—floating across the hotel's brick-walled courtyard or echoing up and down the series of winding stairwells to the fourth floor.

"It sounds just like children laughing," said Benida Cowart, a housekeeper who swears that she and several other staff members have heard the eerie noise. "It gives me goose bumps just talking about it."

A number of guests also have reported hearing the laughter. Some have even said they've seen the children, dressed in late Eighteenth-Century attire and usually attended by a "grandmother" dressed in a long, dark dress and bonnet.

"You hear enough of these stories and you begin to wonder," said Andy Boisseau, a front desk clerk.

He said there are some rooms on the third and fourth floors that housekeepers refuse to go into.

"That got to be a problem," Boisseau noted. "They'd

talk about strange noises and the occasional sighting of what they thought were ghosts—a little boy and girl dressed in Victorian era dress, laughing and playing in the rooms or down in the courtyard with their grandmother not far behind."

Nobody knows how the ghostly trio originated, but one story has it that the children died from scarlet fever while visiting one of the row units in the late Nineteenth Century. The grandmother supposedly haunts the place, too, because she felt responsible for their deaths.

The Linden Row Inn, with its quaint stairways, high-ceilinged rooms, stately corridors, elegant garden and patio, seems the perfect setting for ghost stories. It was here, tradition holds, that Edgar Allan Poe played as a child and was inspired to write his famous love poem, *To Helen.*

The courtyard where Poe played still has many of the same types of trees, bulbs, shrubs and perennial plantings found there in the early 1800s. The inn, built in the mid-nineteenth century, comprises seven row houses—originally ten—with their original plaster cornices, ceiling medallions, marble mantels, handsome stairs and wood-work still intact.

Some researchers theorize the hauntings might be linked to one of several tragedies that occurred when the Greek Revival building served as a popular girls' school operated by Virginia Pegram, widow of famed Confederate General James Pegram. Legend has it that a young girl was killed when she fell from a fourth-floor window.

One story suggests that the ghost—or ghosts—can be traced to the late 1900s when Miss Virginia Randolph Ellett ran a school here.

Jeannette Weir, the inn's French-born general manager, dismisses the ghost stories with a polite chuckle and wave of her hand.

"I do not believe in ghosts," she said one morning over a cup of tea on the patio. "There has to be a logical explanation behind all these strange events. I don't think ghosts have much to do with it."

Try telling that to the out-of-town guest who awoke one night to find sheets hovering about his bed. According to Boisseau, the guest was staying in a courtyard suite when he was awakened by someone—or something—yanking on the sheets.

"It happened three times that night," Boisseau explained. "The third time he looked up and saw the sheets hovering above him. Then the strangest thing happened. The sheets fell down, then he felt a tremendous pressure on his chest, like some small child sitting on him or pushing him down with their hands."

The pressure finally eased, said Boisseau, but the terrified guest then noticed a "shimmering green light" focused on the bedroom wall.

On numerous other occasions, guests on the third and fourth floors have complained of running toilets, slamming bathroom doors, covers flying off beds and bathroom faucets turning on and off.

"The problems always seem to cease when we send the maintenance men to check it out," Boisseau pointed out.

Now listed on the National Register of Historic Places, Linden Row Inn has been perfectly preserved in its Greek Revival style of architecture and today is rated a AAA Four Diamond Inn. In 1988 Linden Row was restored as a full service inn with seventy-one Victorian

style guest rooms, complete with complimentary break-
fasts, color television and a ghost.

THE OCTAGON

Odd- shaped house has eerie history

The old house stands at the corner of a busy intersection in Washington, D.C., nestled among towering oaks and stately rows of cherry trees. From the outside, it's hard to tell that his handsome, well-tended structure situated one block west of the White House happens to be one of the most haunted house in America.

A museum by day and headquarters of the American Architectural Foundation, the two-hundred-year-old Octagon House—so named because of its odd-shaped architectural style—supposedly comes alive at night with dozens of spirits, among them Dolley Madison, the socialite wife of President James Madison.

One of the most persistent ghosts seems to be that of a female slave who, according to legend, was killed by her British lover during the War of 1812 and interred within an unknown wall in the house. Over the years, strange thumping sounds coming from the walls and tunnels beneath the house have been attributed to the ill-fated black woman.

Other restless spirits reportedly haunt the six-sided house as well, including runaway slaves and wounded Union soldiers who died in the house while it served as a hospital during the Civil War.

The unusual, Federal-style home was built in the late 1700s by Colonel John Tayloe, a Virginia planter and friend of George Washington. It was designed by

William Thornton, the architect of the Capitol Building, who named the house The Octagon, even though he gave it only six sides.

The house features include a stunning, oval central staircase, irregularly shaped rooms and closets, and a maze of tunnels which once led to the nearby White House.

The Tayloes and their fifteen children—eight beautiful daughters and seven handsome sons—lived in the house until 1855, with the exception of a period during the War of 1812. The first spirit said to haunt the house was that of one of the daughters.

According to legend, the Tayloe daughters indulged in some stormy love affairs, and the house was often the scene of arguments and broken hearts. One daughter fell in love with a British officer in the early 1800s, but John Tayloe would not allow the man to even enter the house.

One stormy night, after a particularly severe argument with her father, the girl fell down the three flights of stairs to her death. Some say she jumped. Other accounts indicate she tripped and fell. Regardless of how it happened, her anguished spirit was soon spotted flitting about the house, wailing and moaning.

A short time later, Colonel Tayloe moved his family to his plantation in the country. In 1814, following the burning of the White House by the British, the colonel allowed President and Mrs. Madison to take up residence inside the house.

The Octagon House soon became the focal point of Washington's social scene. Dolley Madison, wife of the president, hosted huge and frequent parties during which she adorned the rooms with fresh lilacs, her favorite flower.

After Madison's second term, they moved out and Colonel Tayloe moved his family back in. Much to the colonel's horror, the staircase soon claimed the life of a second daughter. According to tradition, the girl fell while she and her father were arguing about her plans to elope with a suitor the colonel disapproved of. Her ghost, too, is said to haunt the scene of the tragedy.

During the latter part of the Nineteenth Century, numerous witnesses reported glimpsing Dolley Madison's ghost, clad in elegant fashions of the day, and smelling of lilacs, standing or dancing in the entrance hall.

Witnesses also reported seeing the apparitions of footmen attending to ghostly carriages. Other phenomena have been reported over the years, some well into the Twentieth Century—eerie moans, screams, sighs, and clanking of swords, smells of phantom food cooking in the kitchen, the scent of lilacs, and the appearance of human footprints in otherwise undisturbed dust.

Other reports include unearthly smells in the bedroom used by Dolley Madison and ghostly shapes floating through the rear doors to the gardens and walking up and down the staircase.

One of the most frequently reported apparitions is that of a candlelight seen ascending the stairs. As the light reaches the top, screams can be heard, then a sickening thud. Visitors have reported passing through intense cold spots at the foot of the staircase near the exact spot where the Tayloe girls landed.

OLD STONE HOUSE

Historic D. C. home teeming with spirits

In the heart of one of Washington, D.C.'s, most fashionable neighborhoods stands an old stone dwelling that many claim is the most dangerously haunted house in America. For as long as anyone can remember, the house—built in pre-Revolutionary War times by a Pennsylvania cabinet maker—has been center-stage for some of the most bizarre supernatural antics on record.

According to witnesses, unfriendly spirits stalking the gloomy corridors of the steep-gabled structure located at 3051 M. Street, have repeatedly tried to rape, stab and strangle visitors. One victim claims a ghost actually tried to push her over a second-flood balcony.

While some may scoff at such reports, one woman knows better. Her name is Rae Koch. Rae is the park ranger in charge of the house, which was purchased by the National Park Service in 1950 and converted into a museum.

"So far, in the twenty-four years I've been here, I've seen eight ghosts in the house," Rae said. "They're all different kinds, representing all different time periods that the house has been here."

The star performer is a terrifying presence known to the staff as George. George, who inhabits a third-floor bedroom and frequently can be seen wandering along the upstairs hallway, hates women and occasionally gets violent.

He has been accused of trying to strangle women,

knife them, rape them and even push some of them over a railing outside his room or down the stairs.

"There's a ghost in that bedroom who's a real bad guy," Rae explained. "He's one of those self-righteous, you-do-as-I-say types. It's not a nice feeling up there sometimes."

It was Rae, in fact, who claims to have nearly been pushed over a railing by the unseen spirit. Her friend, a respected investigator of paranormal phenomena who spends a lot of time at the old stone house, supported the park ranger's testimony.

"We could sense the presence of the entity," the parapsychologist noted. "It had form. I could feel the thing. Rae was complaining of a pressure on her right side, and I grabbed her and pulled her away from the railing."

Another encounter with "George" almost cost volunteer guide Karen Cobb her life.

"He almost killed me," she explained. "I worked there a number of years, and I had a lot of strange things happen to me. But this was unusual because it was so violent."

According to Karen, the near-tragic incident occurred late one night while she was showing an English friend around upstairs. They had just sat down on a bed when suddenly, "I felt this impression on the bed next to me."

She turned to her friend and asked: "Do you feel that?"

When her friend nodded apprehensively, Karen reached over and became aware of an "ice cold" presence on the bed next to her.

"The next thing I knew, there were hands around my throat, trying to strangle me, like from behind, and I couldn't get loose," Karen explained. "I ended up just struggling and breaking free. I ran downstairs. I ran outside the house, and it was like it was pursuing me till I got outside in the yard."

There, on a pile of bricks outside, Karen collapsed. "My throat was bruised badly. Finally, I got my breath back, and I thought, I'm not going back up there!"

Several visitors—none of whom were aware of the ghostly nature of the old stone house—have complained to management about icy sensations entering their bodies, leading some investigators to conclude they were being "knifed" by some sinister force without actually drawing blood.

Besides "George," witnesses have described dozens of other spirits wandering about the house. They include that of a Civil War-era woman who sits in a rocker on the third floor; a little boy who runs up and down the third-floor hallway; two Colonial Period gentlemen; a young girl with ringlets in her hair; a German-looking craftsman and that of a small black boy.

The ghosts appear to come and go at will, without regard for time of day or night. They stroll down corridors, stand idly by the kitchen fireplace, play on the steep stairwell and occasionally materialize in bedrooms.

Except for "George," none of the other spirits appear to be dangerous.

Rae and other investigators theorize that one of the ghosts is that of Georgetown Mayor Robert Peter who owned the house at the time of the American Revolution. Another ghost haunting the three-story, L-shaped structure might be that of Peter's mistress, for whom the mayor bought the house.

Like most haunted houses, the old stone house has a

long and colorful history stretching back to the mid-eighteenth century. Once thought to be the site of Sutter's Tavern—where George Washington and Pierre L'Enfant laid out plans for the city of Washington—the building has also been used as a private residence, auto body shop and popular bordello.

The handsome old structure has been completely restored and contains much of its original Period furnishings.

PEACHTREE CREEK

Atlanta family stays put in haunted house

The haunting began shortly after Bryan and Rosalyn Drummond moved into their modest bungalow next to Peachtree Creek in northeast Atlanta more than fifteen years ago. It was little things at first—strange footsteps creaking through the house at night, rapping noises in the walls, items falling off shelves or disappearing altogether.

Then it got personal.

"We'd wake up in the morning and find clothes that we had put out the night before scattered across the floor," said Rosalyn, an emergency room nurse at a nearby hospital. "Our toothbrushes would be found in shoes in the closet or toothpaste smeared across the mirror."

"I lost a lot of ties and socks," Bryan, an insurance salesman, noted. "I'd go to look for them in the drawer or in the closet and they'd be gone. Sometimes we'd find them somewhere else in the house, but a lot of time they just disappeared."

The scariest thing happened one night when the ghostly form of an old woman entered their room and sat down on their bed.

"It was incredible," Rosalyn said. "She seemed to come out of the wall and float across the room. She leaned over the bed and smiled at us, then sat down at the foot of the bed. I can still hear the bed creaking and feel the pressure of her hip against my foot."

The Drummonds convinced themselves they had dreamed the whole thing—even though each agreed on details, right down to the old-fashioned dress the specter was wearing and the sad look on her face.

But when eerie moaning noises started waking them up in the dead of night, the couple became convinced something paranormal was behind the strange events in their house.

"The answer was obvious...the place was haunted," Bryan concluded.

At first they were determined to tough it out. No ordinary ghost was going to chase the college-educated young couple away from their home, not after they had spent thousands of dollars renovating the four-bedroom, Craftsman style house built in the early 1940s.

For the next six months nothing happened. No footsteps or banging noises, no strange smells, no eerie ghosts woke them up in the middle of the night.

Then one afternoon the "spirit-like" forms of two little boys dressed in old-fashioned attire suddenly appeared at the top of the stairwell facing the living room. When she saw them, Rosalyn, who was alone at the time, ran out of the house screaming.

Several neighbors came over to investigate and found nothing.

"It was as if they—the ghosts—wanted us and us alone to see them," Bryan later said. "I think they were trying to communicate with us, to tell us something about a past tragedy or some sad occurrence in that house."

They found a paranormal investigator in the yellow pages and invited him for a visit. After combing the house with tape recorders, cameras and heat-sensing equipment, the investigator came away convinced that one or more "supernatural entities" occupied the Drummonds' house.

"He said they were spirits, probably trapped in the house because of some unresolved matter long ago," Bryan explained. "He said we should bring in a medium and hold a séance."

Instead, the Drummonds decided to sell the house.

"We hated to, because we truly loved that place," Bryan said. "But it was getting too much. My wife wouldn't stay there alone anymore, even in the daytime, and we just grew tired of having our sleep interrupted all the time."

They put an ad in the classified section of a local newspaper, advertising it as "One of a Kind Haunted House for Sale. Ghost comes with it."

Two weeks and several calls later, a professor from Kentucky drove down to put in an offer.

"He was moving to Atlanta anyway and felt like the house would fit in nicely with his experiments into the paranormal," Rosalyn said. "The house seemed very important to him. He offered to pay us exactly what we were asking, not a penny less."

Unfortunately, the professor was killed in an automobile accident two days before the house was scheduled to close.

"The coincidence was shocking, and we were devastated," Bryan said. "It was almost as if some higher power was conspiring to keep us in the house."

The Drummonds consulted a priest who convinced them no supernatural involvement was behind the accident.

"He said it was just bad luck," Bryan said.

They decided to keep the house and took it off the market.

"It was the best thing we ever did," Rosalyn pointed out. "Nothing else ever happened. For the past ten years it's been the quietest house in Atlanta. We keep our fingers crossed it will stay that way."

RADIANT BOYS

Ghostly scandal drove famed nobleman
to early grave

On the night of August 12, 1822, Lord Castlereagh, one of England's richest and most powerful men, took a penknife from his desk drawer and slit his throat, killing himself.

The noble's suicide came as a shock to most of the world, but those who knew him weren't all that surprised.

"The wonder of it is that it didn't happen sooner," commented Edward Bulwer-Lytton, an English historian who wrote a biography of Lord Castlereagh.

Some historians think Lord Castlereagh's grim death was foreshadowed by an encounter he had as a young man in Ireland with a so-called "radiant boy." Legend has it that radiant boys are glowing ghosts of boys who have been murdered by parents, usually mothers. Such apparitions are common in European folklore, and might have originated in German myth with the word *kindermorderin*—child murderer.

Radiant boys are usually described as having long, golden hair that resembles a flame, with a slightly orange glow. These lads, who appear to be between 10 and 13 years of age, are said to materialize suddenly, then vanish mysteriously.

According to tradition, the apparitions herald bad luck

and violent death to anyone unlucky enough to see one.

Lord Castlereagh, second Marquess of Londonderry and one of England's most illustrious statesmen, claimed he saw such a specter while on a hunting trip in Ireland.

"Somehow he got lost in the woods and wound up in the lodge of a local farmer," wrote Bulwer-Lytton.

That night he was suddenly awakened by a bright light in the room. Gradually, he became aware of the "glowing form" of a beautiful naked boy, surrounded by a dazzling brilliance. The boy gave him an earnest look and then faded away.

Thinking it was some kind of practical joke, Lord Castlereagh confronted his host the next morning and demanded an apology. The host was aghast.

"What you have seen," said the host, "was the ghost of the boy who has haunted that bedroom for centuries."

The host explained that, according to family tradition, "whoever sees the boy will first rise to prosperity and power and then suddenly die a violent death."

Lord Castlereagh, the second heir in line for his family's fortune, was concerned.

There followed a string of events that left him convinced he was a marked man. First, his older brother drowned in a boating accident. Next, he was caught up in a blackmail scheme by a London gang for sexual transgressions.

According to author Mark Seaman, Castlereagh occasionally enjoyed the company of prostitutes while on parliamentary business in London. One day in 1819, Seaman writes in *The Rest is History*, Castlereagh was approached by a beautiful young prostitute and propositioned. He followed the girl to her room where the prostitute revealed herself to be a boy wearing women's clothing.

"It was a setup," according to Seaman. The moment the boy stripped off his clothes, witnesses rushed in and threatened to denounce him as a homosexual unless he paid them money. In those days homosexuality was a punishable crime and social stigma, so he gave the gang money not to reveal what happened.

"For the next three years, one of the most powerful men in Britain was the victim of continuous harassment by a gang of London crooks," Seaman added. "For Castlereagh, the only escape was death."

Despite his much-heralded success as a soldier and statesman, Lord Castlereagh was a hated man, mostly due to his cold demeanor. In 1821, his father died, leaving not only the family fortune in his name, but also the old man's title.

Soon, Lord Castlereagh's fortunes began to dim. He came down with the gout, contracted a respiratory disease, then was ordered to a sanitarium for observation. Doctors grew increasingly concerned when their famous patient began to show signs of paranonia and dementia.

Eventually, he was confined to his country house and forbidden to have razors or other sharp objects, lest he do something foolish. The house servants were instructed to keep their sick master away from dangerous objects such as knives and forks.

Someone forgot about the twin-edged penknife the master kept on his desk in the study. On the night of August 12, Lord Castlereagh found the knife and cut his throat.

Some say pressures brought on by the blackmail incident combined with his encounter with the radiant boys caused the great man to take his life.

SECOND SIGHT

Nurse feels right at home with spirit world

When Sheri Shannon woke up one night not long ago and saw a ghost sitting at the foot of her bed, she wasn't surprised.

Nor was she really afraid.

The 33-year-old nurse at the Medical College of Georgia in Augusta had seen lots of ghosts in her time, from when she was a toddler. But this was the first time she had actually felt the clammy presence of a spirit so close.

"She was an incredibly old woman, with white hair and wrinkles and a white blouse and Victorian cameo," Sheri said. "When I looked up and saw my feet were actually sticking through her skirt, I jumped up and ran into my mother's room."

The encounter occurred in 1987 while she was visiting her mother at the Partridge Inn, a well-known resort hotel built before the turn of the century. Sheri theorized that the apparition was that of an old woman who had once lived in the hotel.

"She didn't seem to want anything and seemed perfectly at home," Sheri noted. "She smiled at me, but seemed kind of sad."

Sheri's most terrifying haunting experience occurred fifteen years earlier while visiting her father in Arkansas. Late one afternoon she heard what sounded like a big truck crashing into the front of their country house.

"I could hear rocks and debris falling everywhere," she recalled. "I thought, oh, God, somebody's run into the front wall, and ran outside to investigate."

Nothing was wrong. She later learned that the man who previously occupied the house had been killed in a pulpwood accident. She theorized the man's ghost had only come back to re-enact the terrible tragedy.

"A lot of hauntings seem to occur near or at the site where a great accident or tragedy occurred," Sheri said. "That's probably what I experienced—the driver of the truck returning to the spot where it all happened.

She is also convinced that the rambling old house she lives in today is haunted. Her first clue came the day she went with a real estate to look the place over.

"A huge piece of plaster fell off the wall, almost hitting me. I thought, this is not a good sign, not a good sign at all," she said. "There's a ghost here, all right."

The next day her mother, who also is a real estate agent, went with her to look at the house. They couldn't get the front door to open, even though the lock was brand new.

"We tried everything and every key we had," she explained. "It still wouldn't open. It was like somebody didn't want me inside that house."

Other strange experiences followed.

When her baby was eight days old, she noticed that somebody—or something—kept rearranging his clothes and toys. She'd go out of the room for a few moments, only to return and find the baby's clothes completely folded and rearranged.

"I guess the ghost likes him," she said.

She thinks the ghost is that of an old woman who died in the house several years earlier. A neighbor told her the woman's corpse wasn't found until two weeks after her death.

Today, Sheri is so used to the cold spots, strange smells and other signs of ghostly presence in her house that it doesn't bother her anymore.

"I guess she's just an unhappy soul who doesn't know where she belongs," she concluded.

Sheri attributes her paranormal sensitivity to the fact she was born with a caul over her face—a sure sign, she says, that she has the ability to see and hear things others can't.

In folklore, persons born with a caul are supposedly super-sensitive to the spirit world. These people are said to have "second-sight" and are able to predict future events. In some cases, they are also blessed with rare healing powers.

"These things seem like second nature to me," Sheri noted. "I have premonitions, *déjà vu*, all that stuff. It's no big deal to me any longer."

SHERWOOD FOREST

Gray Lady haunts presidential mansion

The house old sprawls in stately splendor beneath the outstretched arms of centuries-old oaks, a stone's throw away from the muddy banks of Virginia's historic James River. Known locally as Sherwood Forest, the house is one of the oldest continuously occupied houses in the country and has been home to two presidents, William Henry Harrison and John Tyler.

For 150 years, it has also been home to one of the Tidewater's most famous specters, the legendary Gray Lady. The present owners, descendants of President Tyler, are convinced something haunts their 44-room mansion.

"It's here, no question about it," said Payne Tyler, whose husband, Harrison, is a grandson of the tenth American president. "Everyone who has ever lived her has heard it."

Legend holds the ghost is the spirit of an elderly woman who cared for a sick baby in the plantation nursery. According to one version of the story, the baby died sometime before 1842, and the old woman's ghost keeps coming back to take care of the child's spirit.

Some say the woman's name was Gray, while others contend the spirit is known as the Gray Lady because of the color of the cloak seen about the apparition. She is said to walk over the creaking floorboards in the hallways, rock in nonexistent rocking chairs and spends time in the corner of the master bedroom.

Payne Tyler learned about the Gray Lady from reading old letters found inside the house when the family restored the plantation in the 1970s. It was during the restoration period that she experienced her first visit from the ghost.

"She disturbed me two times," Mrs. Tyler noted. "I heard her in the next room, but I was not about to open the door. I told her, very politely, that we were going to stay here, she was going to stay here, so we might as well be friends. Then she left me alone."

But she became a firm believer one night in the late 1980s as she slept in the house. Around midnight, she awoke to the sound of someone entering the locked bedroom.

"Someone walked across my room and piddled around in the corner," she said. "You could hear them moving and shuffling things, and I thought it was a burglar. Then they walked over to the foot of the bed and stood there for quite a while and then they went out."

Mrs. Tyler added: "I know all of this really sounds crazy. I would have never believed in a ghost or spirit until I came to live in a house with one. If you live in a house where there's a ghost in it, you believe it."

First mentioned in a 1616 land grant, Sherwood Forest was originally known as Smith's Hundred. The house, built in 1730, is a classic example of Virginia Tidewater design. While most visitors come to view the historic house, its antique furnishings and stately grounds, many come to see the house's famous Gray Lady.

SMURL HOUSE

"Black Form" tormented Pennsylvania family

Not long after the "Amityville Horror" spooked the nation in the early 1970s, a similar outbreak of paranormal activity occurred in the quiet, middle-class town of West Pittston, Pennsylvania. Although less well-known, the so-called Smurl House haunting would make shocking headlines around the world and result in a television movie.

John and Mary Smurl fell in love with the small duplex house the moment they laid eyes on it. It was small but had plenty of room for themselves on one side and their son, Jack, and his wife, Janet, and two daughters, Dawn and Heather, on the other.

Built in 1896, the house needed a lot of work. But that posed no problem for the Smurls who went to work painting and touching up where necessary. Described as a "close, loving, good Catholic family," the Smurls soon had the place in perfect shape.

Then strange things started happening in Jack and Janet's section. Unexplainable claw marks showed up in the bathroom and unusual stains were found on the newly installed living room carpet. Weird noises, levitations, foul odors and ghostly visitations plagued the bewildered family. They described it as "like a nightmare."

Jack's TV burst into flames. Water pipes leaked mysteriously, even after repeated soldering. Toilets flushed for no reason, radios turned on and off, even when unplugged. Heavy footsteps were heard tramping up and down the stairs and across the attic. Drawers opened and closed when no one was in the room.

It wasn't until 1985 that the first visual manifestation occurred. A black, human-shaped form appeared to Janet in the kitchen. The form, which stood about 5 feet, 9 inches tall and had no facial features, dematerialized through the wall.

The hauntings increased. A large ceiling light fixture crashed down for no apparent reason. On the night thirteen-year-old Heather was to be confirmed, Jack felt himself lifted into the air by unseen hands.

Frightened and bewildered, the Smurls asked the Catholic Church to intervene. Only when their request was denied did the Smurls being in a team of psychic researchers to investigate. Ed and Lorraine Warren, the same husband-wife team who had investigated the Amityville haunting, determined that demonic forces inside the house were being activated by the daughters' approaching puberty. Prayer sessions were constantly interrupted by growling voices that warned them to "get out of this house!"

The investigation revealed that "at least" four spirits haunted the house, one of them probably a demon.

At that point the Smurls decided to take their story to the newspapers. Soon after they appeared on a TV talk show, the Roman Catholic Diocese of Scranton took action. The Reverend (now Bishop) Robert F. McKenna went to the house, said Mass in Latin and performed more than fifty exorcisms.

But the hauntings continued. The TV set emitted an eerie glow. Mirrors shook and cracked. Janet was punched and slapped by unseen hands. Jack saw the ghosts of two women dressed in Colonial dresses—and was sexually attacked by a scaly, succubus-like creature posing as a beautiful woman.

The demon would allow the Smurl family no peace. When the family went on a camping trip to the Poconos, the demon went along. A "pig-like creature" that stood on two legs followed Jack around, even one day to work.

In 1977, twin daughters—Shannon and Carin—were born. By now the Smurls were growing weary of the unexplainable disturbances and thought a move might be order. But moving apparently would do no good, as the demon threatened to follow them wherever they went.

In the summer of 1985 the temperature in the house dropped below freezing. Obscene voices were often heard, along with strange, cracking sounds. Several times a "roaring voice" shouted Janet's name from the basement.

The eerie happenings became more frequent—and more dangerous. The family dog was yanked into the air by mysterious hands. One of the little girls was thrown from her bed, and the sound of hissing snakes was heard.

Right before Christmas 1986, Jack again saw the black form. The banging noises continued, in spite of more exorcisms, as did terrible smells and the violence. Other manifestations were seen, including "shadow people" that sometimes appeared without warning.

The Smurl family's ordeal eventually brought swarms of reporters and curiosity seekers. They went on television and gave newspaper and magazine interviews to tell their story. The publicity confirmed suspicions held by some that the haunting was a hoax and that a book or movie deal might be behind the whole thing.

Sure enough, the Smurls' experiences became the subject of a book—*The Haunted*—published in 1988, followed by a movie released in 1991.

The Smurls stayed in the house for twenty-five years. In 1989 they finally sold the house and moved away. The paranormal activity stopped.

SPECTRAL FLEET
Ghost ships stalk U.S. destroyer

After several months' duty in the Pacific, the crew of the destroyer *U.S.S. Kennison* was looking forward to a few days of shore leave in San Francisco.

"We were tired," recalled Seaman Howard H. Brisbane, "and all the boys were thinking about was liberty and their girlfriends."

On the morning of September 15, 1942, as the ship made its way through the fog toward the Golden Gate Bridge, Brisbane was standing watch near the bridge when he heard a series of faint hissing noises, followed by creaking and popping sounds.

"Something was making a huge, splashing sound," he recalled. "But the fog was so thick it was hard to see anything."

The fog lifted, and he saw the outline of a ship.

"It was an old-fashioned sailing ship, the kind with two masts and lots of rigging," the seaman added.

The ship appeared to be unmanned. Other sailors aboard the *Kennison* also saw the strange ship, including torpedoman Jack Cornelius, who was stationed near the fantail. It was Cornelius who notified the bridge about the strange sighting.

"You saw a what?" the officer on duty asked.

"A ghost ship, Sir," Cornelius replied. "It's on a course of one-three-five relative. It's somewhere on the starboard quarter."

"That's odd," the officer fired back. "The radar scope

is empty."

Except for a brief report filed in the ship's log, nothing more was made of the strange sighting. Then, five months later, in April 1943, Brisbane and other *Kennison* crewmen saw another "ghost ship."

"We were approximately fifty miles west of San Diego and were returning to port after convoying the troopship *Lurline*, Honolulu-bound through the submarine belt," Brisbane said. "Carlton Henschel and I were on the 2000-2400 lookout watch on the flying bridge, enjoying the night."

During a "slow sweep" of the horizon with binoculars, Brisbane saw the "curling, white bow wake" of a vessel off starboard bow. Frocusing above the wake, he made out the silhouette of a Liberty freighter.

"Ship out there," he told Henschel.

"Yep, got her," Henschel replied. "Radar has been probably tracking her for twenty miles and the OD (officer on duty) is just waiting to chew us out if we don't report it."

When the officer checked with the radar operator, however, the scope was blank.

"We did not challenge the vessel by signal light or radio because it was Navy policy not to challenge presumably friendly ships encountered outside the war zone," Brisbane noted. "But I kept tracking the ship with binoculars, and by using a trick of night vision—focusing my gaze to either side slightly, never directly at the freighter—I could see it with the naked eye."

Then something incredible happened.

"The ship vanished," Brisbane declared. "I had been tracking it for a full thirty seconds, then nothing, poof, it was gone."

The officer on duty then ordered a 360-degree search of the horizon. Empty ocean. Empty radar screens.

Now, twice the *Kennison's* lookouts had sighted strange vessels that vanished from sight in scant seconds.

"Ghost ship" sightings have been reported for centuries. From 1831 to 1865, some three-hundred such apparitions were recorded in the logs of various American ships.

"I don't have the answer," Brisbane concluded years later in a magazine interview. "But as a witness to two such sightings, I say the evidence defies logical explanation."

SPLASHY POLTERGEIST

Family couldn't escape watery demon

It began one rainy night in October 1963, just when the Francis Martin family of Methuen, Massachusetts, had settled down for a quiet evening of TV.

A few minutes into the program, they noticed a small damp patch forming on the den wall between two book-shelves. The spot grew quickly from the size of a nickel to that of a large dinner plate.

"That's odd," Francis Martin remembered telling his wife as he got up to investigate the curious spot.

His first thought was that a pipe had frozen and burst. But that didn't seem possible since it was only early October. Nor did a drain backup seem likely either, since he'd had the system cleaned out only a few weeks before.

As he ran his fingers across the sticky surface of the wall, he wondered what could have caused the strange spot. His wife and children joined him, and soon they were oohing and aahing over their mysterious discovery.

Then came a loud popping sound, "like a small-cal-iber pistol being discharged." A split-second later, a spout of water burst from the wall.

"It pretty much drenched us," Martin told a reporter. "The water was freezing cold. It was the coldest water I've ever felt."

Seconds later, the gushing spray of cold water

stopped. After cleaning up the mess, Martin promised his wife he would phone the plumber first thing in the morning.

The next day, however, another spot appeared on a different wall. Soon, a fountain of water was pouring in, forcing the family to rearrange furniture to keep it dry. As before, the mysterious stream of icy water lasted about twenty seconds before suddenly stopping.

After several days of popping sounds and mysterious fountains of water—usually occurring every fifteen minutes at various places—the Martin house was so much awash that they moved into the home of Martin's mother-in-law in Lawrence, not far from Methune. Unfortunately, the water gremlin pursued them to Lawrence, and in a short time five rooms in the mother-in-law's place were drenched too.

"Water was everywhere," Martin recalled. "The walls, carpets, furniture, everything was soaked."

The deputy fire chief was asked to investigate, and the house was checked for leaky pipes. There were none.

At least one official—a deputy named Mains—was present when a jet of water suddenly burst through a plaster wall and shot two feet into the room. He also heard the curious popping sound.

"It was like a nightmare," Martin told the press. "If I didn't know any better, I'd think some kind of water demon was after us."

Rather than inflict their problem on his mother-in-law any longer, the family returned to their home. This time, the water supply was turned off at the main, and the pipes were drained.

Their first night back home nothing happened. Then, next morning, another wall exploded in a shower of ice-cold water. Then another, and another.

In the days that followed, damp spots continued to appear, and walls would erupt with streams of water at the same time, none of them lasting longer than twenty seconds.

Once again the house became unlivable, and, once again, the Martins returned to Lawrence. But, just like before, the "water demons" followed, eventually forcing them to return home.

"It was if whatever was causing the problem was ordering us back home," Martin noted. "It wouldn't tolerate us leaving our home."

The watery assaults gradually came to an end. A few more spots appeared, but no more leaks or showers shot forth from the walls.

To their dismay, the Martins never discovered the source of their "watery haunting." How—or why—gallons of water would suddenly jet from the dry plaster walls of their house would remain a mystery.

Equally perplexing was the gradual cessation of the phenomenon.

"Moisture buildup" was the official explanation. To this day, however, no official has been able to explain how moisture buildup can result in showers of icy water gushing forth for twenty seconds, then stopping.

One psychic investigator theorized the bizarre activity was the work of a poltergeist—a kind of troublesome ghost that delight in wreaking havoc in the lives of mortals.

"This particular poltergeist probably favored working with water," the investigator theorized. "It was a true water demon."

ARTHUR STILWELL

Unseen companions guided railroad tycoon

Young Arthur Stilwell's parents were stunned when he walked into the house one day and announced that he had quit his low-paying job and planned to move out West with his new bride.

They were even more surprised when he told them why: Ghostly voices inside his head had commanded him to give up his job and head West.

In the West, the voices told him, "you will find your destiny. You will truly become one of the nation's great captains of industry."

Stilwell moved west, just as he had been commanded by the voices, built a railroad and became one of America's richest and most powerful tycoons. He also found success as a writer, churning out more than thirty books, all of them bestsellers.

In what has to be one of the eeriest testimonials on record, the millionaire author would later credit his success to the strange voices inside his head.

But the mysterious voices that had instructed him to move west were nothing new to young Stilwell. In fact, the voices had been with him for as long as he could remember, guiding him and instructing him along life's way.

As a 4-year-old child, he had once remarked to his mother: "I like the people in my head, but they make me so angry sometimes because they won't come out and let me see them."

Later, he told his mother not to worry about his "unseen companions" because they meant no harm.

"They're just like you and Dad," he said. "They tell me all sorts of wonderful things. They've even told me what I'm going to do when I grow up."

While still a youngster in school, the same voices had told him he would grow up and marry a girl named Jennie Wood. Even more compelling was their prediction that he would marry the girl within four years!

At the time he had never even heard of Jennie Wood. But four years later, after having met the girl at a party, the couple indeed became husband and wife.

The eerie voices stayed with Stilwell for the rest of his life. In time they formed such an integral part of his personality that he couldn't have kept them a secret even if he had wanted to. And, as he made millions building railroads and cranking out one best-selling book after another, he enjoyed delighting his friends and family members with stories about his "unseen friends."

His road to fame and fortune had opened up that morning at his parents' home when he announced that he and Jennie were moving to the Wild West town of Kansas City. It was there, he told them, that the voices had urged him to go; it was there, he said, that he would make his fortune.

Finding a job in Kansas City was easy. It wasn't much, hardly a fortune, but his $30 salary at a local brokerage house enabled him and Jennie to settle down peacefully in what both thought would be a life of domestic bliss. Then, out of the blue, the voices came to him again, advising him what to do next.

Stilwell, who had already begun to write stories and dream of making money in business, relayed the information to his wife.

"I am to build railroads," he said.

"Railroads?" Jennie gasped. "But how? With what? We have no money."

The soon-to-be-millionaire couldn't answer his wife's questions. The truth was, he hadn't the foggiest notion how to put together any kind of business, let along a complex, expensive operation like a railroad. Besides, where would he get the money? Railroads required enormous sums of planning and capital.

With no money in his pocket and no family wealth to draw from, how on earth was he going to do it? Could the voices have made a mistake this time?

The answer came to him in a flash—backers! He would ask wealthy men to pump start-up capital in the project. Surely, he reasoned, there were sufficient numbers of wealthy men around who might be willing to risk a few dollars on helping him build a railroad.

The next day he started calling on potential investors. Within weeks he had managed to put together a small group of investment partners whose infusion of money enabled him to launch the Kansas City Belt Line Railroad. The line would later expand into a sprawling network of rails that covered 15,000 miles of track.

As the railway grew, so did Stilwell's remarkable success as a writer. Year after year, as new lines opened up under his control, he cranked out a steady stream of best sellers. Arthur Stilwell—rich, famous, handsome and happy—soon became the toast of the western literary and business world.

In 1900 he was busy putting together new plans to construct a railroad linking Kansas with the Gulf of Mexico when the voices came to him again. This time they told him to stop construction at once, that danger and a "cloud of disaster" lay ahead.

Without hesitation, Stilwell re-routed the terminal line from Galveston, Texas, to a mosquito-infested wasteland that would later be named Port Arthur in his honor. On September 8, 1900, a mighty hurricane slammed into Galveston, nearly obliterating the city.

Stilwell had listened to the voices and narrowly averted the "cloud of disaster" they had warned him about.

Never once did he doubt the wisdom of the voices again. In 1910, based on information provided by his "unseen companions," he predicted World War I. He also prophesized the defeat of Germany, the rise of Hitler, the collapse of the Russian czar and the rise of communism.

In 1928 the voices spoke to him one last time. Lying on his deathbed, he took his wife's hand and urged her to be strong.

"The voices have been telling me again to protect you," he whispered. "You must be brave and try not to join me too soon."

This time Jennie ignored both her husband and the strange voices inside his head. Two weeks after his funeral she jumped to her own death from a New York skyscraper, some say summoned by her late husband's mysterious voices.

SURRENCY
HAUNTING

They saw and heard things "not of this world"

Herschel Tillman was only 8 years old the first time his daddy took him to see the ghost.

"It was on a Sunday, right after church," the 85-year-old retired postal carrier recalled in an interview. "My daddy drove us out to the old Surrency House in an old buggy. We went inside and saw and heard things not of this world."

Some of those things included a clock that chimed 13 times, then spun mysteriously backwards, boots that marched around the room, plates and cups that jumped off tables and soared through the air on their own, and an eerie, scratching sound that seemed to come from within the old walls.

The biggest shock came when a shower of "hot bricks" fell onto the front porch from out of nowhere.

"That place was haunted, there's no two ways about it," Tillman concluded. "There must have been at least a dozen ghosts inside the Surrency house."

The Surrency house, a rambling, two-story structure that once served as a railroad hotel in the tiny town of Surrency in Appling County, was reputed to be the most haunted house in America. In its heyday, from 1885 to 1925, some 20,000 curiosity-seekers—including newspaper reporters, clergymen and scientists—flocked there to observe the strange goings-on.

The two-story house was built by Allen Powell Surrency who settled the area in the 1850s when most of the swamp and pine forests of Appling County were unclaimed. He operated a sawmill, while Mrs. Surrency opened the house to travelers, especially those riding the train on the Macon to Brunswick line.

Sawmill workers and travelers from all parts of the state enjoyed the small-town hospitality and ambience of the boarding house. Their favorite activity was to sit up late swapping stories about "wild haunts" and strange critters said to roam the woods late at night.

The Surrency House's reputation as a gathering place to swap ghost stories spread far and wide. Visitors from all parts of the county would ride over in wagons to hear the latest stories. They especially delighted in hearing tales about ghosts and "spook lights."

After watching several ink bottles leap from a table and listening to unearthly screams inside a bedroom, one reporter from the *Savannah Morning News* wrote: "The whole house is clothed in darkness and…bears the spirit of the supernatural."

That same reporter said he watched the hands on a clock "move around with exceeding rapid motion…It would pause and strike oddly, and this went on for seventeen minutes."

A reporter from the *Atlanta Constitution* said fire logs kept rolling out of the fireplace while books mysteriously fell off shelves. The reporter fled the house when several hogs and chickens suddenly appeared in the living room from out of nowhere.

Stories about the Surrency haunting appeared in newspapers as far away as Russia and Greece. Dozens of books were written about the phenomena, and it soon became the most celebrated haunted house in America.

Phillip Dukes, who ran a local grocery store, remembers stories handed down by his grandmother about the house. "She used to spend the night there often, because she was Mrs. Surrency's sister. A lot of times when she put her shoes under her bed at night, she'd wake up next morning and find them out in the hallway. That happened so many times she came to expect it every night."

According to the late Reverend. Henry Tillman, the supernatural forces haunting the Surrency house rarely disappointed visitors. Tillman said his father often described how objects in the house would dance on the table at mealtimes, bedcovers would roll up and down at night, and glowing red eyes would hover over the railroad tracks directly in front of the house.

"My daddy was one of the most honest men who ever lived," Tillman said. "When he said he saw those things, he really saw them."

Eager to rid their home of their unnatural guests, the Surrency family—for whom the town is named—sought the help of scientists, ministers, mediums and psychics. But efforts to drive away the ghost—or ghosts—were unsuccessful. If anything, they seemed to make matters worse. Windows suddenly began to shatter at random, doors refused to stay closed—even when locked—and scissors and irons flew wildly across rooms.

Tradition has it that a murder was behind the Surrency haunting. One story says that a railroad worker was killed outside the home, and it was his spirit that plagued the house and its occupants until the old house went up in flames in 1925.

But another version holds that owner Allen Surrency himself was to blame because he was rumored to be in league with the devil. One witness recounted how Surrency once demonstrated his arcane powers by running a stick completely through his hand without spilling a drop of blood.

According to tradition, the ghost—or ghosts—continued to torment the Surrency family long after they had moved to another home.

"That thing haunted Old Man Surrency until the day he died," commented one old-timer. "But when he was buried, the haunting stopped."

SYMPHONIC SPIRITS

Composer inspired, tormented by "tide of music"

Robert Schumann, the great German composer, was having a bad day. Twice in one morning he had tried to commit suicide—once with an open blade, the second time by throwing himself into the Rhine River near Bonn. The first attempt was thwarted by a nurse at the asylum where he was confined.

"Why don't you let me die in peace?" he reportedly shrieked at a pair of fishermen who plucked him out of the river after his second attempt failed.

He wanted to die, he said, to escape "evil inner voices" that had tormented him since childhood.

In the beginning, the voices had been kind to the gifted young musician born in Saxony in 1810. He was only 12 when they came to him, whispering in a language not of this earth. As an adult, he called them "spirits of the voice," but as a child they were always giving him advice and warning him of impending danger.

The voices helped him publish his first composition at the age of 12, a simple accompaniment to the 150th Psalm. They also helped him write and publish plays, poems and translations of classical verse.

At first he was afraid of the strange murmuring. They came to him at night, when he sat alone at the piano, struggling to find the right note. He described them as "soft sounds, gentle whisperings that ran fingers deep within my brain."

Soon, the voices seemed to take control of his music. They urged him to write more, play more, perform more. At the same time they warned him never to ignore them, never forget that they were in total command of his spirit as well as his music.

By the time he was 30, Schumann, the son of a working class bookseller, was a famous—though not necessarily rich—man. When friends like Chopin and Brahms inquired as to the origins of his music, the deeply sensitive composer and poet always claimed that "the angels in my head" provided themes and melodies.

In 1840, Schumann married Clara Wieck, the beautiful young daughter of his piano teacher, who would go on to become a famous pianist in her own right. The artistic couple had stormy moments, yet managed to produce eight children.

The next few years were productive, as the Schumann's traveled to Russia and Austria, where Schumann received critical acclaim for his First Symphony in B-flat. During this busy period he helped many talented friends, including Mendelsohn and Brahms, by giving them favorable reviews in a musical magazine he published.

It was also during this time that he composed many of the solo songs, or *lieder*, on which his reputation was built. Friends referred to that year—1840—as the Year of the Song because Schumann wrote more than 100 songs.

Again, the inspiration was attributed to his inner voices—the "angels" in his head that whispered to him sweet tunes and melodies at night.

In 1844, Schumann suffered a nervous breakdown. He found that he could no longer focus on musical ideas. The voices were growing too loud, getting out of control, seemingly wanting to take over his life.

Then, suddenly, the voices went away. He moved to Dresden, a thriving musical center, and began working furiously. The next year, still living in Dresden, Schumann penned his famous *Symphony Number Two in C Major.* He was overjoyed at the thunderous reception he received!

Then the hallucinations returned—more painful than ever—and he sank into a deep depression. In constant pain and fear of his sanity, the great artist was unable to work for months. To make matters worse, his old friend, Brahms, had moved into his house and—some say—began a torrid love affair with his wife.

By 1852, he was complaining of "strange afflictions of hearing"—a repetition, apparently, of nonstop tonal sounds. As his mental condition worsened, Schumann sought solace in seances. In vain he tried to communicate with the spirit world, to try to better understand his supernatural torment.

In 1853, the Schumann's participated in a "table rapping" session—a phenomenon that was all the rage in Europe. According to notes left in his diary, Schumann was convinced that tables could "move" and "rap out" rhythms to songs. "I said, 'Dear table, play the opening theme to my C minor Symphony,' and it tapped it out…"

The tide of music began to drown him. No longer soft and gentle, the sounds in his brain became bitter, threatening. Then one day the "sweet voices" of the angels returned, softly urging him back to work.

Schumann told a friend that the music inside his head was "fully formed and complete." The sound, he said, "is like distant brasses, underscored by the most magnificent harmonies. This must be how it is in another life, after we've cast off our mortal coil."

One night Schumann told his wife that the angels were calling out to him to enter their world. Then, without further warning, those same warm entities became "terrifying demons" that beckoned him to join them in hell.

In 1855, Schumann checked himself into an asylum at Bonn, a medieval village on the Rhine River. The next year, the day after a visit from his wife—her only visit to see him in the asylum, in fact—he choked on some food and finally passed over into the realm of the angels.

TOWER OF LONDON

Ancient landmark stained with blood of innocents

For almost a thousand years, the Tower of London has been the scene of more bloodletting than any other single structure in Europe. More people have been tortured and executed here than in all the dungeons of England, France, Germany and Italy combined.

It seems only natural, then, that this grim landmark situated in the heart of London should also be considered one of the most haunted. Millions of tourists descend on the ancient complex each year, many of them completely unaware of the Tower's cruel past—or the number of ghosts said to walk its lonely corridors.

"This place is stained deep with the blood of martyrs and innocent people," said T. Lace McDonald, a British historian and author of several articles about the Tower's infamous past. "It somehow seems fitting that the spirits of some of those unfortunate souls should return to this place of horror."

Built in 1078 by William I—better known as William the Conqueror—the Tower, situated on the site of an ancient Roman fortress, grew to become one of the most awe inspiring and frightening buildings in the world. That one word—Tower—was enough to send shudders down the spines of otherwise fearless invaders or political enemy.

While most of those who faced the executioner's axe or rope were commoners, thieves, rebels and traitors, many were judges, priests, kings, queens and other titled nobles who had fallen out of political favor. The ghost of William Wallace, the famous Scot rebel who was tried at the Tower before being drawn and quartered at nearby Smithfield in 1305, supposedly walks the grounds late at night.

One of the most famous early spectral encounters occurred in 1241 when several priests saw the ghost of Sir Thomas Becket, seventy-one years after his murder in Canterbury Cathedral. The archbishop's spirit apparently objected to expansion work being carried out on the grounds and struck the new walls with a cross, causing them to crumble to the ground.

The most frequently reported wraith is that of Queen Anne Boleyn, the second of King Henry VIII's wives who was beheaded in 1536. Before dying, she reportedly whispered that she would return from the grave to torment her accusers.

The queen's ghost has been seen by dozens of Tower staff and guardsmen patrolling the grounds. One sentry was knocked unconscious by "white bolts of fire" after he tried to stop the queen's spirit for questioning. Several other guards witnessed the event.

Anne Boleyn's ghost is said to carry her head under her arm on the eve of a death. A sergeant serving with the Artist's Rifles was on duty the night before several spies were due to be executed during World War I. He claimed that the night before Carl Lody was executed, he saw the ghost of Anne Boleyn in a silk dress and a white ruff.

Anne has also been seen in the Tower Chapel. On

one occasion, a young guard supposedly saw a ghostly procession marching down the aisle. The guard testified that Anne Boleyn, clad in a Tudor-style dress, led the group of specters.

On Feb. 12, 1957, a group of guardsmen reportedly saw a "shapeless white ghost" on top of the tower. Ironically, it was on that same day in 1554 that 17-year-old Lady Jane Grey was beheaded on Tower Green, after only a nine-day reign as queen.

Two other ghosts of beheaded women haunt the Tower as well. Catherine Howard, another hapless wife of Henry VIII, has been seen several times, as has Margaret Pole, countess of Salisbury.

The 70-year-old countess met a particularly horrendous end in 1541 when her executioner's axe failed to hit her neck on his first three attempts. On the fourth attempt the blade only wounded the countess, who jumped up and tried to escape before she was caught and restrained. It was the fifth and final blow that finally sent her head rolling.

Because of the particularly gruesome manner in which she died—screaming and struggling between each swing of the executioner's axe—it should come as no surprise that Countess Margaret's ghost has become a familiar sight on the Tower grounds. Her cries of terror are reportedly heard regularly on the anniversary of her death.

Other ghosts seen in or around the blood-stained Tower include King Henry VIII, who is often seen floating in mid-air, the Duke of Northumberland, Sir Walter Raleigh and two young princes—Edward V and Prince Richard—brothers who died as children in 1483 when their uncle wanted them out of his way to claim the throne as King Richard III.

The skeletal remains of the two small boys were found stuffed in a wooden trunk behind a dilapidated stairway in an abandoned section of the Tower in 1674. While historians generally disagree whether their uncle was really behind the gruesome double murder, it is clear he had most to gain by their deaths.

Visitors and guardsmen occasionally hear childish laughter near the area where their broken and mutilated bodies were found. Other Tower officials claim they have heard similar laughter in the bedroom where, legend has it, Richard III had them suffocated with a pillow before dismemberment.

Their ghosts, like those of countless other victims of the executioner's axe and rope, still wander the gloomy Tower, their chill laughter and haunting images forever etched in supernatural lore.

DICK TURPIN

Legendary highwayman
still terrorizes backcounty

Of all the infamous highwaymen who terrorized Eighteenth-Century Britain, none was more notorious than Dick Turpin, a dashing, handsome psychopath whose bloody deeds remain a favorite topic of tavern conversation.

To some, Dick Turpin was a swashbuckling hero, a Robin Hood who robbed from the rich and gave to the poor. But to others, especially hard-pressed lawmen from London to Glasgow, he was Britain's most notorious criminal, an out-of-control rogue who slaughtered innocent people and stopped at nothing to stuff his pockets with ill-gotten booty.

Turpin was the ringleader of a group of bloodthirsty bandits known as the "Knights of the High Toby," who specialized in waylaying solitary travelers along lonely roads. His victims—who probably numbered in the thousands—were sometimes brutally tortured before being executed.

One man who refused to hand over his money promptly died a horrible death when he was tied to a tree and set on fire. Turpin and his band supposedly laughed at the man's tortured screams as they galloped away into the night.

But when the infamous highwayman was captured near York in 1739 and sent to the gallows, thousands of supporters turned out to mourn his passing. Women swooned, children blew kisses and even the executioner supposedly shook hands with the condemned criminal.

It is said that before throwing himself off the ladder to his death at the end of the rope, Turpin bowed gallantly to the ladies and promised his spirit would return from the dead.

"You shall see me again, of that you can be certain," he shouted to the startled crowd.

Perhaps it was that cryptic vow to return that triggered countless sightings of Turpin's ghost. Even today, his shade reportedly haunts the lonely highways of Essex, North London and Yorkshire.

He has been seen in so many locations that nowadays any spectral vision on horseback is usually said to be that of Dick Turpin riding up from hell.

Nearly every country inn, restaurant, pub and old home in the region has a tale or two about the highwayman haunt. Some say he still rides the night wind astride a fiery black horse, wearing a black tri-corned hat.

The specter has been seen as far away as the Midlands, but his favorite haunt is near Woughton-on-the-Green, a tiny village near London. Witnesses say the figure is cloaked and hazy and "moves restlessly about as though waiting for something to happen."

The Old Swan Inn in Woughton-on-the-Green has been the scene of numerous sightings. Legend has it that Turpin stopped there once and forced a blacksmith to shoe his horse backwards, to elude pursuers.

Turpin's ghost also is said to haunt the A-11 highway between London and Norwich, especially a stretch north of Loughton through Epping Forest. The ghost, mounted on a black horse, gallops down Traps Hill with a thin woman clutching at his waist, her feet dragging the ground.

Those who have investigated the story say the haunting is tied with Turpin's brutal act toward an old, wealthy widow who lived near Loughton. He waylaid her and tortured her until she revealed the whereabouts of her jewelry, then tied her to a horse and dragged her to her death.

Perhaps the most fascinating story associated with Dick Turpin's ghost has to do with Heathrow Airport. The airport, one of the busiest in the world, is located in Hounslow Heath, an area not far from London that was once plagued by Turpin's highwaymen.

Turpin reportedly returns occasionally in phantom form to startle and sometimes frighten airport personnel.

Born in Essex in 1706, Richard Turpin mastered the art of petty thievery as a young boy. The son of a small farmer and pub manager, it is said he stole eggs from widows and candy from children. One report said he went to church not to pray, but to snitch money from the tithing bowl.

In time, Dick Turpin became the most feared highwayman and robber in all of England. The king sent soldiers after him on numerous occasions and offered a substantial reward for his head.

Legend has it he became a popular folk hero with the rural population. Claims that he robbed only from the rich and gave to the poor have never been substantiated, but there seems to be some truth to reports that he was fed and sheltered against the king's men by friendly peasants in the East Anglian countryside.

In 1739 Turpin's reign of terror finally came to an end when a tip led to his capture near York. Convicted and sentenced to death, the legendary rogue shaved, donned a new outfit and went to the gallows with a smile on his face.

MARY LURANCY VENNUM

Child's spirit torn between two worlds

One cold winter night in 1878, a tall, distinguished-looking gentleman clutching a small black bag climbed down from his horse-drawn carriage and was quickly ushered through the front door of a handsome, elegantly appointed house in the small town of Milford in eastern Illinois.

A sense of urgency filled the spacious, well-lit home as the dapper visitor was rushed up the winding flight of stairs to a bedroom at the far end of the hall.

From beyond the bedroom door came an eerie mixture of sounds—the unmistakable laughter of a child interspersed by wild, animalistic grunting.

"This way, please," the teary-eyed host explained, leading the way.

Dr. E. Winchester Stevens took a deep breath, then followed the host and a friend of the family named Roff into the room.

As a long-time physician and psychic researcher, Dr. Stevens had encountered some rather bizarre cases in his time. But all his years in medicine hadn't prepared him for what awaited him amid the flickering shadows of the gloomy, Victorian-styled bedroom.

On the high, four-poster bed crouched a pretty young girl, about thirteen, clad in a long, ruffled nightgown. The girl was obviously in a great deal of pain. She hissed and screeched and made meowing sounds like a cat.

"She's been like this for weeks," the girl's father, Robert Vennum, said sadly.

Suddenly the girl's mouth opened. Two spirits, both girls, started speaking through her. Their conversation lasted more than an hour, after which the teenager passed out and fell to the floor.

Dr. Stevens woke the girl and helped her back to bed. Then, after putting her in a deep trance, he took the girl's hand and said, "Tell me what's troubling you, child. Perhaps I can help you."

For several minutes, Dr. Stevens listened patiently while Mary Lurancy Vennum recounted an incredible story. In a clear, steady voice, interrupted at times by wild shrieks, she told the doctor how for the past three years, ghosts had visited her room on a regular basis— first in her dreams, then more and more while awake.

"What kind of ghosts?" the doctor asked.

"They weren't just ghosts," Mary replied. "I saw heaven and angels and a lot of other ghosts who talked to me just as you are talking to me."

The girl went on to explain how the "ghosts" who came to her were dead people she had known in life— aunts, uncles and other deceased relatives. But the ghost that frightened her the most was that of a young woman named Mary Roff who wanted to control her."

"Mary Roff!" the family friend exclaimed, rushing to the side of the bed. "That is my daughter. Why, she has been in heaven twelve years now!"

Roff quickly explained how his daughter had died several years earlier at the age of eighteen, having been tormented by epileptic seizures throughout most of her life. Roff, who had never before believed in ghosts, suddenly felt his skepticism wane.

Was it possible, he wondered, that the spirit of his late daughter was returning from the grave to take over Mary's body?

Indeed, Mary Lurancy Vennum was giving every sign of being "Mary Roff" and was constantly asking to be allowed to go home with her father.

"Then let her come," Roff urged the doctor and Vennum.

On February 11, "Mary Roff" moved to the Roff household. Meanwhile, Dr. Stevens learned more about the girl's troubled past—about how one night she had awakened screaming in her sleep: "There are persons in my room," she told her parents, "I feel their breath on my face."

A few days later she had another seizure, followed by another, then another. She began to "speak in tongues" and complained that one particular spirit, that of "Mary Roff," was trying to take control of her body.

That was when Dr. Stevens, of Janesville, Wisconsin, was brought in by the family for consultation.

After "Mary Roff's" arrival in her new home, she recognized furniture, friends, photographs, clothes—even the family pet. She was also quick to recall past events—events only family members could have known about.

A few months later, Mary Vennum's personality emerged. "What am I doing here?" she asked, then begged to be taken home.

But no sooner had she spoken than "Mary Roff" returned and took control. Over the course of the next several days, the dead girl's spirit returned no less than a dozen times.

On May 21, "Mary Roff" announced she was going away and gave the body back to Mary Vennum. The departed spirit promised she would return some day, but not for a long, long time.

Mary Lurancy Vennum returned home and was never bothered by ghosts again. Occasionally, she would visit the Roff home and "allow" the spirit of Mary Roff to speak through her to her parents. The parents accepted the arrangement, because it gave them an opportunity to communicate with their long-dead daughter as if she were alive.

'MAD ANTHONY' WAYNE

Revolutionary hero's phantom re-enacts famous ride

———

The ghost of one of America's most famous Revolutionary War heroes supposedly haunts the lonely lakes and forests of upstate New York.

Over the years, hundreds of people have reportedly seen the gloomy specter of Major General Anthony Wayne, one of George Washington's favorite generals, who went on to earn fame by crushing Indian resistance in the Northwest Territory at the Battle of Fallen Timbers on August 20, 1794.

Nicknamed "Mad Anthony" because of his daring military exploits against the British, his ghost is often seen riding the midnight wind on his beloved horse, Nab, wearing a cloak, high boots and a tri-cornered hat.

The sightings usually occur immediately before or during thunderstorms, leading many to believe the ghost is re-enacting a 1779 ride to warn Revolutionary troops at Storm King Pass that the British were coming. Wayne braved a ferocious thunderstorm and midnight gallop through the mountains to rally his troops and lead them in a spirited bayonet charge at Stony Point.

Other people have seen Wayne's ghost at Fort Ticonderoga, which he commanded before surrendering it to British General "Gentleman Johnny" Burgoyne in

1777. The specter is often seen hovering in the dining room of the commandant's quarters, or sitting in a wing chair before the fireplace.

Some observers claim the specter smokes a church warden pipe and drinks from a pewter mug, copying the pose in Wayne's portrait hanging on a nearby wall.

Wayne's phantom also is said to roam the wooded shoreline of Lake Memphremagog, which he and two Canadian guides visited in 1776 for the purpose of capturing eagles to train for hunting. Not long after his death, local Indians and settlers claimed to have seen his ghost, dressed in buckskins and moccasins, walking along the lake's shore with an eagle perched on each shoulder.

Born on New Year 's Day 1745, in Chester County, Pennsylvania, Wayne's fascination for the military developed at an early age. The son and grandson of famous generals, his first experience as a battalion commander proved disastrous when he led a campaign against the British in Quebec.

In following years, however, the hot-tempered, impetuous brigadier general went on to earn fame and glory in battle after battle. His daring exploits and unpredictable battlefield tactics helped earn him the nickname, "Mad Anthony."

After the Revolutionary War and the Indian wars that followed, Wayne returned to Philadelphia as a hero. In the fall of 1796 he was stricken with gout. The next month, on December 16, he died. At his request, the 51-year-old conqueror was buried in a plain oak coffin near Erie, Pennsylvania.

Not long after his death, explorers, settlers and others along the frontier started seeing Wayne's ghost. In the early 1800s, a group of trappers swore they saw the dead general's apparition floating across a lake with "his feet barely touching the water." Later, the same group said they saw the old general standing by a tree staring at them.

In addition to his prowess as a battlefield commander, Wayne was widely regarded as a ladies' man. One old flame, Nancy Coates, became so distraught because of the general's roaming eye that she threw herself into a lake near Wayne's headquarters at Fort Ticonderoga and drowned.

Ever since, Nancy's ghost has been seen in and around various parts of the fort, sometimes running along the densely wooded paths around the lake. Several witnesses reported seeing the dead woman floating face-up in the cold waters.

Some who have heard the ghostly wailing claim she is crying out for her long-dead lover.

Wayne's phantom has also been spotted roaming Valley Forge National Military Park on his horse. Some say they've seen his ghost near a statue erected in his honor at Brandywine Battlefield.

There is a macabre ending to Wayne's legacy. More than a decade after his death, son Isaac Wayne decided to move his father's body to the family burial plot at St. David's Church in Radnor, Pennsylvania. Young Wayne recruited an old friend of his father to go with him in a one-horse sulky to fetch the remains.

When the general's body was dug up for removal, however, it was discovered that his corpse was remarkably preserved. There was no decay at all, except in the lower portion of one leg. That presented a problem, since the plan had been to dismember the skeleton so that it could fit in the back of the sulky.

The dilemma was solved by dissecting the body and boiling the flesh from the bones in a large iron kettle. The cleaned skeleton was then taken back home in the sulky for a proper burial. The rendered flesh and the knives used in the grisly operation were replaced in the original coffin and re-interred in the old grave.

WHITE HOUSE

Ghostly parade of residents past

On the night of May 27, 1955, President Harry S. Truman went on national television to reveal a shocking secret. While an estimated 50 million Americans looked on, the president told interviewer Edward R. Murrow that a ghost stalked the drafty corridors of the White House.

It was no ordinary ghost, either.

"I think it's the ghost of Abraham Lincoln walking around," the president said calmly into the camera. "Perhaps he's here to warn me about something."

Ever since his arrival at the White House eight years earlier, Truman said he had been bothered by a strange tapping noise on the other side of the presidential bedroom door. The sound, described as "unusually sad and melancholy," usually came to him late at night or early in the morning.

Most often it happened around 3 a.m. while the rest of the White House slept. As the president told it, he'd be awakened by the knocking sound beyond the door. He'd crawl out of bed, fling open the doors and peer down both sides of the hallway.

The results would always be the same—nothing.

"There was no one there," he explained. "So I'd go back to bed."

In bed he'd think about all the old legends, about how the spirit of Lincoln—who was 55 years old when struck down by an assassin's bullet—prowled the dark halls of the White House, moving from room to room, a tormented look in his eyes and a plaid shawl draped around his craggy shoulders.

In life, Lincoln was a man surrounded by death—first his son, Willie, then the hundreds of thousands of men in blue and gray who fell during the Civil War. Long before his assassination, Old Abe had experienced startling premonitions of his own death. Ten days before he was shot by John Wilkes Booth, he dreamed of a president killed by an assassin.

According to some biographers, Lincoln also had visions about other unworldly events, a gift supposedly handed down to him by his psychic mother. Night after night, disturbing and significant symbols and premonitions came to him in his sleep, and he found that he was greatly troubled by his conscience.

Among the things Lincoln claimed to have seen was "the knowledge of and...the power to change the future."

As a youth growing up in a backwoods log cabin near Hodgen's Mill in what is now Larue County, Kentucky, Lincoln felt it wiser to keep his psychic powers to himself. But just about everybody who knew him was aware of the ill-fated president's amazing ability to "see" into the future and predict events without knowing how.

The gift apparently ran in the family. Robert Todd, the president's oldest son who went on to become a statesman and lawyer, seemed haunted by a series of associations with presidents that ended tragically. He was with his father at Ford's Theater the night he was shot and happened to be in the company two other presidents when they were shot by assassins—James A.

Garfield in 1881 and William McKinley in 1901.

Never again would Robert agree to meet—or even be near—a president. Invitations to subsequent presidential functions were ignored.

Shortly before his election in 1860, President Lincoln saw a strange face next to his in a mirror. His wife, Mary Todd Lincoln—who also claimed to have the gift of prophecy—believed it was a premonition of a tragic future.

"You will be re-nominated for a second term," the First Lady predicted, "but you will not live to see its conclusion."

Edwin Stanton, a close friend and member of Lincoln's cabinet, once confided: "I have known that the president is not like other men, and that he believes that the future can be seen now and that the afterlife is for repentance. It would not surprise me if, when he dies, his spirit refused to leave the White House and that it remains there, restless and troubled, until it feels that the last of these 'sins' has been paid for."

Far-fetched and fanciful though this seemed, it began to make sense to Harry Truman some ninety years later as he pondered the mysterious spectral visitor outside the presidential bedroom door. The more he read about Lincoln's alleged psychic abilities and the series of ghostly visions the late president claimed to have had while in the White House, the more convinced Truman became that Lincoln's tormented spirit still haunted the White House.

Many other visitors to the White House claimed to have encounters with a ghost matching Lincoln's description, including Eleanor Roosevelt, who often sensed the dead president's presence, usually at night while she was writing. The Roosevelts' dog, Fala, would bark excitedly for no apparent reason.

The first official sighting was made in the 1920s by Grace Coolidge, wife of Calvin Coolidge. She reportedly saw the president's spirit standing by an Oval Office window looking across the Potomac. Queen Wilhelmina of Holland also awoke one night in the White House stateroom and fainted when she found herself staring into the face of the late president.

To the end of his days in 1972, Truman believed that whoever was president and whoever lived in the White House would also hear the discreet rapping on the bedroom door and perhaps would someday have the opportunity to communicate directly with Lincoln's ghost.

After Truman's presidency, the ghost seemed to disappear, only to return with the arrival of Ronald Reagan. The president's daughter, Maureen, reported seeing a "transparent man" in various rooms in the White House. At least one other guest saw the dead president sitting on the bed, putting on his boots.

Except for the Reagans, no other administration has admitted to any encounters with the famous ghost.

Female ghosts have also been seen in the White House, including Abigail Adams, wife of the second president. Visitors and staffers have reported seeing her spirit wandering through the East Room with arms full of laundry. Dolley Madison, who planted the Rose Garden, has also made several appearances.

Another apparition often observed wandering the corridors at 1600 Pennsylvania Avenue is believed to be that of a British soldier killed during the War of 1812. Some say the specter, last seen in the mid-1950s, appears sad and carries a torch.

WINCHESTER HOUSE

Eccentric heiress worked hard
to keep "bad" spirits away

For nearly four decades, Sarah Winchester went to sleep
each night with the sound of saws and hammers echoing
through her lonely old house on the outskirts of San
Jose, California. As long as there was noise, she could
sleep. As long as the clatter and bang of men at work
reverberated throughout the sprawling, eight-story mansion, she could rest peacefully in her four-poster bed,
knowing she would live another day and that the "bad
spirits" would stay away another night.

But, let the racket slack up for one moment, and she
was wide awake, shouting at the top of her lungs for the
army of carpenters she employed day and night to get
back to work.

That was how it had been for the melancholy old
woman since 1884, the year the wealthy widow moved
from her palatial home in New Haven, Connecticut, to
an eight-room farmhouse in the Santa Clara Valley,
California. Ever since, she had been obsessed with her
peculiar destiny—to build and build in order that the sins
of her late husband would be wiped clean and she would
find peace once again.

Sarah Winchester's torment had begun shortly after
the death of her beloved husband, William Hirt

Winchester, inventor of the famous Winchester repeating rifle that had won the Wild West. In despair, she had turned to spiritualism for comfort.

During a séance with Boston medium Adam Coons she was told that, unless she spent all of her husband's money expanding and constantly renovating her house, she would never know peace. That was the only way she could atone for the thousands of people who had been slain by her husband's rifle.

"The souls of the victims killed by the rifles made by your husband—and there are thousands of them—seek revenge," the medium told Winchester. "Your life will be cursed unless you buy a house, enlarge it, and continue building to it for the rest of your life."

The loss of her husband was the second major tragedy to befall the once-beautiful belle of New Haven. In 1866, one year after her celebrated marriage to the founder of Winchester Repeating Arms Company, Sarah's infant daughter died from a respiratory ailment. The death of her only child left the young mother grief-stricken, teetering on the brink of madness.

Then, on March 7, 1881, her husband died from pulmonary tuberculosis. Sarah inherited William's vast fortune, but her wealth did little to ease her grief. A friend suggested she seek the advice of a spiritualist—a common course of action in those days. The trip to the spiritualist—and the series of seances that followed—would change the young widow's life forever.

"Your husband is here," Coons told Sarah at a séance. "He says for me to tell you that there is a curse on your family, which took the life of he and your child. It will soon take you, too. It is a curse that has resulted from the terrible weapon created by the Winchester family.

Thousands of persons have died because of it and their spirits are now seeking revenge."

He advised Sarah to withdraw her substantial fortune from the bank and move to California. There she would be guided by her husband's spirit.

"You must start a new life," she was told. "You must build a new home for yourself and for the spirits who have fallen from this terrible weapon, too. You can never stop building the house. If you continue building, you will live. Stop, and you will die."

As long as there was the sound of hammering in the house, she would not be troubled by the evil spirits. Her instructions were to add on to the house constantly, to expand, renovate and rebuild, day after day, night after night. She must fill her ever-growing home with a cacophony of rasping saws and clattering hammers and groaning pulley systems.

Sarah did as she was told. For the next thirty-eight years, until her death in 1922, Sarah Winchester—one of the richest women in America—spent six million dollars and ended up with a house of 700 rooms, 950 doors, 40 bedrooms, 47 fireplaces, 40 stairways, 52 skylights and 10,000 windows. She engaged hundreds of architects, designers, carpenters and other workmen, many of whom labored in relays, to see the project through.

No expense was spared. One door imported from Europe cost $800, while thousands were spent on several art glass windows. One room had four fireplaces and four hot-air radiators. In a climate where temperatures rarely came close to freezing, she had five separate central heating systems installed.

There seemed no end to the nightmarish project as convoys of wagons shipped in supplies on a daily basis.

She even had a railroad line constructed on the property to help haul in timber, bricks and other equipment.

Room after room was added to the rapidly expanding maze of hallways and stairways. Entire wings were built overnight, only to be torn down the next day and started all over again under Sarah's supervision. Skylights were installed, as were trap doors and towers. Doors were put in that led to steep drops to the lawn below.

The number 13 was ever-present--the greenhouse had 13 cupolas, the walls had 13 panels and many of the wooden floors contained 13 sections. Every staircase but one had 13 steps. Convinced that the "bad spirits" dwelled in cupboards, Sarah had them made in awkward shapes, sizes and positions so the spirits within would lose their way. Eventually, 2000 cupboards were installed, some of them only one-inch deep.

Still not content with her grotesque creation, Sarah ordered craftsmen to build a series of fake roofs and balconies to which there was no access. Pillars were placed upside down in several rooms. Miles and miles of wire ran throughout the house, connecting push-button communicating devices that were unfathomable even to the men who installed them.

Every night at midnight she retired to her "Blue Room" to convene with the spirit world. A bell would ring, summoning phantom entities that would proceed to tell her what her next task would be. To prevent evil spirits from entering her home, she designed numerous blind passageways, fake doors and windows. She tried to stay one step ahead of the spirits by sleeping in a different bedroom each night.

Sarah treated the good spirits royally, often holding lavish banquets in their honor. Thirteen places would be set in the main dining hall—one for herself and twelve for selected ghosts. Real people were rarely invited to her home, and she even turned away Theodore Roosevelt and Mary Baker Eddy. One of her few guests was the great illusionist Harry Houdini, who never spoke of his single visit to the Winchester home.

Through it all, the occult-inspired homeowner surrounded herself with gangs of servants and butlers. Most were easy to hire, but, understandably, difficult to keep. As new chambers were added on, the household staff found it increasingly difficult to find their way about the maze.

In 1922, the spirit-cursed millionairess felt chest pains but refused to accept the fact she was dying. Instead, she ordered her laborers to work harder and faster, to make even more noise than before in order to drive off the evil spirits coming to claim her soul.

On September 4, she conferred with the spirits of the house one last time, then retired to her bedroom. Sometime during the night she died. For the first time in nearly four decades, the entire house fell silent. The next morning, the workmen put down their tools out of respect.

For the next sixteen years, the gloomy old house remained empty. Not a creature stirred within—no housemaid, carpenter, or evil spirit. In a place once filled with the harsh clatter of hammers and saws, silence now reigned supreme.

Eventually, permission was given to open the estate to the general public as a museum. To this day, however, there are some parts of the house that have never been fully explored. There are doorways and stairways leading to chambers yet unknown, entire wings that remain undisturbed in the silent shadows.

Over the years, visitors and employees have reported strange encounters, ranging from ghostly footfalls and banging doors to mysterious voices and windows that bang so hard they shatter. Balls of light have been seen, as well as a gray-haired female apparition floating along dark corridors and through walls in several of the halls.

Visitors have heard organ music and whispering voices. Some observers complain of "cold spots" in the house, a sure sign, say experts on the paranormal, that spirits are present.

Most are convinced that the ghost of Sarah Winchester walks the lonely old mansion—a sad, weeping specter said to be searching for her lost baby and beloved husband.

WOMAN IN BLACK

Female phantom struck terror
on streets of Roanoke

The streets of Roanoke, Virginia, were haunted in the spring of 1902 by a mysterious "woman in black" who struck terror in the hearts of all who laid eyes on her.

Hundreds of people, mostly men, reportedly saw the female phantom during her month-long "reign of terror." Newspaper reports described her as "tall and handsome," with "dancing eyes" and always clad in a long, black cloak.

"She was as beautiful as evil itself," one witness was quoted as saying. "I shall never forget that face for as long as I live."

Exactly why the phantom was so feared is a mystery in itself, since there is no record of her having harmed anyone. Still, women kept their children indoors by day, and men hurried home from work at night.

"Her name was on every lip," wrote the *Roanoke Times*. "Strong men trembled when her name was spoken; children cried and clung to their mothers' dresses; terror reigned supreme."

Who was this woman of dark intrigue, and where did she come from? Nobody really knows, but L.B. Taylor Jr., an author who investigated the case, says the people of Roanoke were convinced she was a ghost.

"She would suddenly appear before someone in broad daylight," Taylor said. "She would talk to the person, then vanish."

The situation became so grim, Taylor added, that "brave men refused to even look at a strange woman on the street for fear she'd be the phantom."

One encounter, as reported in the *Times,* involved a prosperous young merchant on his way home about midnight. The woman in black suddenly appeared, calling out his name.

"The woman was only a couple of feet behind him," the article said, "and he naturally increased his pace faster and faster. But the woman gained on him, finally halting him in the middle of the sidewalk and placing a cold, clammy hand upon his shoulder."

At that point, the article noted, the young man "dashed off to his house, flew inside and locked the door and kept it locked all night."

At the end of March the citizens of Roanoke breathed a deep sigh of relief when it appeared that the woman in black was gone. Soon, however, there were reports of a similar apparition in other nearby towns and cities.

In far-off Nebraska, a similar apparition stalked the streets of Alma. According to one newspaper account, "The spirit form of a young woman is walking our streets...She exudes from the depths of some dark alley and rushes past lone pedestrians."

One male witness said he saw it "vanish in the moonlight." Another said he was chased by the ghost which "whistled and sang" to him as he ran through the streets.

About the Author

E. RANDALL FLOYD is a nationally syndicated newspaper columnist, motion picture screenwriter and best-selling author of several books, including *Deep in the Heart, The Good, the Bad and the Mad: Weird People in American History* and *100 of the World's Greatest Mysteries: Strange Secrets of the Past Revealed.*

A former European correspondent for United Press International, he worked for *The Florida Times-Union* and the *Atlanta Journal-Constitution.* He later lectured at Georgia Southern University and Augusta State University.

Mr. Floyd offers talks on a number of topics, ranging from strange and unusual aspects of Civil War history to historical oddities and the paranormal. He lives in Augusta, Georgia, with his wife, Anne, and their son, Rand.

To contact Mr. Floyd to arrange lectures, guest appearances, autograph signings, or to order books, please call the Augusta office at (phone & fax) 706-738-0354, or write: Harbor House, 3010 Stratford Drive, Augusta, Georgia 30909. Email: harborbook@aol.com.

OTHER BOOKS
BY

E. RANDALL FLOYD

100 of the World' s Greatest Mysteries	$16. 95 Deluxe Trade
The Good, the Bad and the Mad	$19. 95 Deluxe Trade
Deep in the Heart	$24. 95 Deluxe Trade
America' s Great Unsolved Mysteries	$24. 95 Hardback
Great Southern Mysteries	$16. 95 Hardback
	$ 9. 95 Deluxe Trade
More Great Southern Mysteries	$16. 95 Hardback
	$ 9. 95 Deluxe Trade
Great American Mysteries	$16. 95 Hardback
	$ 9. 95 Deluxe Trade
Ghost Lights and Other Encounters with the Unknown	$16. 95 Hardback
	$ 9. 95 Deluxe Trade

Please add $4.95 shipping and handling for the first book, $2.50 for each book thereafter.

To order, send your request to:

HARBOR HOUSE
3010 STRATFORD DRIVE
AUGUSTA, GEORGIA 30909
706. 738. 0354
harborbook@aol. com

Please allow four weeks for delivery of your order. Mr. Floyd will autograph all ordered books. Please indicate how you would like each inscription to read.

ATTENTION: COLLEGES, UNIVERSITIES, QUANTITY BUYERS
Discounts on these books are available for bulk purchases.
Write or call for information on our discount programs.

SOURCES AND ADDITIONAL READING

Alexander, Marc. *Haunted Pubs in Britain and Ireland*, Sphere Books Limited, London, 1984

Bell, Art, and Steiger, Bard. *The Source: Journey Through the Unexplained*, Paper Chase Press, New Orleans, 1999

•Bord, Colin and Janet. *Unexplained Mysteries of the 20th Century*, Contemporary Books, Chicago, 1989

Clark, Jerome. *Unexplained*, Visible Ink, Detroit, MI, 1999

Cohen, Daniel. *The Encyclopedia of the Strange*, Dodd, Mead & Company, New York, 1985

Godwin, John. *Unsolved: The World of the Unknown*, Doubleday & Company, Garden City, NY, 1976

Guiley, Rosemary Ellen. *The Encyclopedia of Ghosts and Spirits*, Facts on File, New York, 1992

Hauck, Dennis. *Haunted Places*, Penguin Books, New York, 1996

Hill, Douglas, and Williams, Pat. *The Supernatural*, Signet Books, New York, 1965

Holzer, Hans. Ghosts: *True Encounters with the World Beyond*, Black Dog & Leventhal Publishers, New York, 1997

Holzer, Hans. *Yankee Ghosts*, Bobbs-Merrill Company, Indianapolis, 1966

Ingram, M.V. *Authenticated History of the Famous Bell Witch*, Clarkesville, TN, 1894

Jones, Denice. *The Other Side: The Boy Who Sees Ghosts*, New Horizon Press, 2000

Jones, Louis C. *Things That Go Bump in the Night*, Hill & Wang, New York, 1959

Kubler-Ross, Elizabeth. *On Death and Dying*, Macmillan, New York, 1969

Lemming, Davis. *The World of Myth*, Oxford University Press, New York, 1990

Lowndes, Marion. *Ghosts That Still Walk*, Alfred A. Knopf, New York, 1941

Moody, R.A. Jr., M.D. *Life After Life*, Bantam Books, New York, 1985

Myers, Arthur. *The Ghostly Gazetteer*, Contemporary Books, Chicago, 1990

Platnick, Kenneth, *Great Mysteries of History*, Dorset Press, New York, 1972

Randles, Jenny. *The Paranormal Source Book*, Piatkus, London, 1996

Readers Digest Association. *Facts & Fallacies: Stories of the Strange and Unusual*, Pleasantville, NY 1988

Readers Digest Association. *Mysteries of the Unexplained*, Pleasantville, NY, 1982

Readers Digest Association. *Strange Stories, Amazing Facts*, Pleasantville, NY 1977

Scherts, Helen Pitkin. *Legends of Louisiana*, New Orleans Journal, 1922

Shuker, Karl. *The Unexplained: An Illustrated Guide to the World's Natural and Paranormal Mysteries*, Carlton Books Limited, London, 1996

Smith, Suzy. *Prominent American Ghosts*, The World Publishing Company, Cleveland and New York, 1967

Theisen, Donna and Matera, Dary. *Childlight: How Children Reach Out to Their Parents From the Beyond*, New Horizon Press, Far Hills, New Jersey, 2001

Time-Life Books. *Ghosts: The Enchanted World*, Alexandria, VA

Time-Life Books. *Mystic Places*, Alexandria, VA, 1992

Tutt, Keith. *Unexplained Natural Phenomena*, TV Books, New York, 1997

USA Weekend. *I Never Believed in Ghosts Until...*, Contemporary Books, Chicago, 1992

Warren, Ed and Lorraine. *Graveyard: True Hauntings From an Old New England Cemetery*, St. Martins Press, New York, 1992

Wilson, Colin and Wilson, Damon. *The Encyclopedia of Unsolved Mysteries*, Zachary Kwintner Books, Ltd., Chatham, Kent, 1987

Wilson, Colin. *Afterlife-An Investigation of the Evidence for Life After Death*, Grafton Books, London, 1985

Wilson, Colin. *The Psychic Detectives*, Pan Books, London, 1984

Wilson, Colin. *Unsolved Mysteries*, Contemporary Books, 1992

Zavala, Adina de. *History and Legends of the Alamo and Other Missions in and around San Antonio*, Arte Publico Press, Houston, 1996